D1712289

Crossing the Border

*An Introduction to the Practice of
Christian Mysticism*

Crossing the Border

*An Introduction to the Practice of
Christian Mysticism*

Russell M. Hart

Templegate Publishers
Springfield, Illinois

Published in the United States of America in 1993 by:
Templegate Publishers
302 East Adams Street
P.O. Box 5152
Springfield, Illinois 62705

Manufactured in the United States of America

ISBN 0-87243-197-5

Dedication

To my parents, Milfred and Myrtle Hart, with great affection

Acknowledgements

To the many people who made this book possible, I express my gratitude: the members of the intercessory prayer group of Rockville United Methodist Church, Harrisburg, PA; those who shared their journey with me who now await the resurrection: Nora Bergstresser, Maxine Rotz, Margaret Shiffer Long, Ivan Park, Mildred Stintzcum, Lorna Frutiger and Marian Billet; and my two colleagues in ministry who read the manuscript and made suggestions: Dr. John Piper Jr. and Dr. Jay Wesley House.

Thanks are due to the following publishers for the use of quoted material:

Leech, Kenneth *True Prayer: An Invitation to Christian Spirituality.* © 1980. Harper/Collins.

Leech, Kenneth *Soul Friend: The Practice of Christian Spirituality,* © 1980 Harper/Collins.

Jackson, Edgar N. *Understanding Prayer: An Exploration of the Disciplines and Growth of the Spiritual Life.* © 1968. Harper/Collins.

The Way of the Pilgrim. © 1965. Harper/Collins.

Underhill, Evelyn *Mystics of the Church.* James Clarke & Co. Ltd. © 1925. First American edition, Morehouse Publishing Co.

Underhill, Evelyn *Worship.* © 1936. Crossroad Publishing Co.

Brown, Raymond E. *The Churches the Apostles Left Behind.* © 1984. Paulist Press.

Walsh, James, S.J. (ed.) *The Cloud of Unknowing.* © 1981. Paulist Press.

Luibheid, Colm & Russell, Norman (trans.) *John Climacus: The Ladder of Divine Ascent.* © 1982. Paulist Press.

Maloney, George, S.J. *The Prayer of the Heart.* © 1981. Ave Maria Press.

Fedotov, G.P. *A Treasury of Russian Spirituality.* © 1950. Sheed & Ward, London.

Table of Contents

PRELIMINARY

FOREWORD

This book was first intended to be about the practice of prayer, but became one about the practice of Christian Mysticism. Perhaps it would be more accurate to say that true prayer must inevitably lead to a direct experience of the presence of God, and this—for lack of a more precise word—must be called "mystical." Evelyn Underhill puts it this way: "The Christian mystic...is one for whom God and Christ are not merely objects of belief, but living facts experimentally known firsthand; and mysticism for him becomes, in so far as he responds to its demands, a life based on this conscious communion with God."(1)

The subject of mysticism is widely misunderstood both within and outside the church. At the very least, it is perceived as any vague, dreamily-romantic sense of the "spiritual." At worst, one senses the whiff of superstition and the stench of the occult. Joseph Fletcher put this misconception in the simplest possible terms when he remarked that mysticism is a word that begins in mist and ends in schism.

From the beginning of my ministry I have been aware of a few individuals in every congregation I have served, who were of a "mystical" bent, and who claimed to have a direct intuition of the presence of God. Although none of these people were radical, or disruptive of church order, I didn't quite trust them. They were usually unconventional and not strict "denominational loyalists" in the sense I might have preferred. They were often unpredictable and usually prophetic. In various forms and degrees, they sought to be in constant communion with God, and to conduct their affairs in order to please Him.

Another reason I didn't quite trust them is because this first-hand knowledge of God always eludes definition. Such claims are subject to verification only as the receiver demonstrates evidence of a surren-

13

dered life. Because everyone is subject to human frailty, this "proof" is not always obvious. Hence, one can easily draw the conclusion that the mystic is deluded.

Another reason I didn't quite trust them is because the mystic way, being one of self-surrender, tends to raise "red flags" in the brains of armchair psychologists, of which I was one, and which abound within the ranks of the clergy.

And yet, a quarter-century of the practice of ministry had taught me that Christianity must be experiential, or it is nothing. Without persons who "feel" their religion, the church would die a cold, intellectual death. Christian mystics are "...the eyes of the Body of Christ."(2) Yet, apart from the church, mystics are susceptible to delusions, superstitious practices, and the occult. These pursuits are extremely dangerous, for—as one of my mentors once put it—"every spirit ain't the Holy Spirit."

The seeds of a mystic consciousness were planted early in my own life. My mother may have been largely responsible for this, although my paternal grandmother also had a deep and abiding faith in Jesus as a real person. The seeds may have been planted early, but they landed on rocky ground. Frustration with the practice of ministry, a serious illness, a dramatic healing and my own need for Christ may have pulverized the formerly unyielding soil.

There were other seeds as well. Most everyone in my generation read J.D. Salinger's *Franny and Zooey*. Franny introduced me to the Pilgrim and the Jesus Prayer. I flirted with the discipline of the Prayer for awhile, but it proved demanding—too taxing for one not given to introspection.

And yet, years later, when I finally read *The Way of the Pilgrim*, it was like meeting an old friend. This simple man, tramping through the Russian countryside with only a sack of dry bread, the Jesus Prayer and the Philokalia, seemed to be seeking to impart to me a peace that I desperately needed. My subsequent reading of the *Philokalia*—a collection of texts from the Eastern Fathers—seemed like a homecoming after a long journey. Many of these names will probably be new to the reader: Marcarius of Egypt (ca. 300-390), Hesychius of Jerusalem (d. 432-3), Diadochus the Blessed (ca. 450), Isaac the Syrian (7th Century), and St. Simeon the New Theologian (d. 1022), to name a few. These masters of mystical theology testify to the presence of God within the deepest self.

A thorough rereading of the words of Evelyn Underhill (1875-1941) followed, this time with new eyes. During this same period I was also introduced to the works of Metropolitan Anthony Bloom whose synthesis of dogmatic and mystical theology is presented in a way that is truly pastoral.

Through the influence of these persons, I not only found that the emphasis of my book was changing, but also that I was sifting through my store of memories of persons to whom I have ministered, and who have ministered to me. I began to realize in a new way that their practice of Christianity would have been impossible but for the sense of the mystical presence of God in their lives. I found also that their contributions to my spiritual journey required inclusion in this book. Thus, any resemblance between persons living or dead and the persons mentioned in this book is not coincidental, but entirely deliberate. Their mention is my expression of gratitude.

This book is intended for those who would develop their own mystical sense along the way of their faith journey. It is not intended for those who would continue the journey alone, apart from the fellowship of believers which is the church. Neither is it intended for persons who are reluctant to express their love for the Creation, which may yet become God's good world.

(1) Underhill, Evelyn, *Mystics of the Church*, Morehouse-Barlow, Wilton Connecticut, Copyright, James Clarke and Co. Ltd., 1925, p. 10.

(2) *Ibid.*, p. 12.

TO BEGIN

Whenever I am asked to conduct a workshop on the practice of prayer, the request invariably carries with it the accompanying stipulation that it be "useful." I think this means that for many people prayer seems an esoteric activity that does not really intersect with life as it is actually lived. More than a little of the theologizing about prayer that takes place in pulpits across the land does seem to border on the esoteric. "Give us something we can actually use?" is the essential question about prayer, for prayer is life itself, and as essential as breathing. A life without prayer is truly a life without meaning. I hope that these chapters will prove as useful for the reader as their writing has been for me.

The Eastern Orthodox branch of the church has always insisted that before there can be a theology of prayer, there must be the practice of prayer. If we in the Protestant tradition—clergy and laity—are to approach living prayer, we may have to begin to "put the heart before the course." This means that we must first struggle with the practice of prayer before we begin to theologize about it.

My seminary education provided a coherent, systematic, and comprehensive theology of prayer. Trouble was, my prayer life was frequently stalled—so frequently in fact that most of the time it was non-operational. Perhaps this illustration will clarify what I am trying to say.

Several summers ago my family and I traveled up the Red River of the North on a paddle-wheel steamer. As we wound through the city of Winnipeg, Canada, we passed under an abandoned railroad trestle whose swing-section was stuck in the same direction as the river's flow. The bridge was a white elephant even when it was dedicated seventy-five years ago because it was built to allow the passage of freight ships that the railroads had even by that time put out of business.

17

The paint was scarcely dry before the bridge jammed in its swing position, and as no one knew how to repair it, it was simply abandoned. The railroad hurriedly constructed a stationary replacement several hundred yards upstream, and the life and commerce of the city quickly resumed. The abandoned structure became a haunt for pigeons and the butt of jokes. The structure is still impressive, but it faces in the wrong direction to be of any use.

So it was with my prayer life, I thought. I, too, had been facing in the wrong direction. Before there can be living prayer, there must be repentance, which in Greek—curiously enough—is "metanoia" or turning. Attentive prayer connects us with the Father. Attentive prayer is the direction toward God of all the attention of which we are capable.(1) It is the rejection of every thought which is not God!

Living prayer has two aspects which Evelyn Underhill identifies as habit and attention. Habit is doing something in a systematic and regular way until one's life would seem incomplete without it. Attention is paying attention to an idea so long and so well that we can continue in that state no matter what we are doing. Each aspect has a weak and a strong point, as Underhill continues:

"Habit alone easily deteriorates into mechanical repetition, the besetting sin of the liturgical mind. Attention alone means, in the end, intolerable strain...Habit tends to routine and spiritual red tape; the vice of the institutionalist. Attention is apt to care for nothing but the experience of the moment, and ignore the need of stable practice, independent of personal fluctuations; the vice of the individualist. Habit is a ritualist. Attention is a pietist."(2)

Together, habit and attention contribute to a state of stability and peace, and also detachment from feelings and thoughts. Metropolitan Anthony Bloom, perhaps Eastern Orthodoxy's most eloquent exponent of the practice of living prayer, gives us an illustration of the state of prayer where the "bridge" connects the one who prays and the One to whom one prays:

"A Moslem's family used to keep a respectful silence whenever he had a visitor but they knew that they could make as much noise as they wanted when he was praying, because at such times he heard nothing; in fact, one day he was not even disturbed by a fire that broke out in his house."(3)

The state of prayer, however, is not something that can be switched on and off like an electric light. One must prepare for the state of prayer through a preliminary state called meditation which is "a disciplined way of thinking, an ascetical exercise marked by discipline and sobriety. It involves pursuing one line of thought and renouncing all others."(4)

Several years ago I took swimming lessons at the YMCA. My goal was to be able to swim seventy-two lengths, or one mile, every day. My problem was that as soon as I submerged, random thoughts swarmed through my brain. As a consequence, I would swim seven or eight lengths and lose count. When I asked the coach how I might better concentrate, she replied, "It's really quite simple. Every time you lose count, start over!"

Metropolitan Anthony says in this regard:

"Whenever we begin to think of God, or things divine, of anything that is in the life of the soul, subsidiary thoughts appear; on every side we see so many possibilities, so many things that are full of interest and richness; but we must, having chosen the subject of our thinking, renounce all, except the chosen One. This is the only way in which our thoughts can be kept straight and go deep."(5)

Meditation, then, is preliminary to prayer. While meditation consists of thoughts focused upon God, prayer is the rejection of every thought in order to stand face to face with God.

Attentive prayer is wordless prayer. This may be hard for those who grew up in Protestant churches to understand, for our worship tends to be linear and cerebral—in a word, wordy! Words are, however, important! Jesus responded to his disciples' request for instruction on how to pray by teaching them the Lord's Prayer. Words are appropriate in prayer as long as they enable us to focus our attention upon God. When we focus upon God and not the words themselves, we approach living prayer. When the focus returns to the words again, prayer returns to meditation.

For years I prepared for prayer by imagining Jesus to be in the room with me. The Eastern Fathers, however, were convinced that the richer the image, the less real the presence. Why? Because an image—even a mental image—is an idol that obscures the real presence. It is a confusion between the idea of God and God Himself. In the Orthodox East, the illuminative way is described in terms of darkness. This means that "the clearer the light shines, the more it blinds and darkens the eye of the soul. It is a deepening of life in faith and faith is essentially trust in the unseen power of God."(6)

19

Our hearts cry out for something more tangible than this, but this we must simply reject. At the Transfiguration, Peter wanted to build three booths, one for Moses, one for Elijah and one for Christ. He and his companions wanted to hang on to the Holy through some object or token. When we were children we may have captured fireflies in a jar, thinking that whenever we had a need for wonder and delight we could retrieve the jar from under our bed and experience the fireflies all over again. Yet what did we always find? Dead fireflies! We must lay aside our cherished idols, for until we do this, God will not be able to get out from behind the image that we have created to take His place.

To meet God face to face is always a time of judgment for us. The god we may have learned about in Sunday School, the one who "walks with me and talks with me" is the same God who awed Isaiah in the Temple. There are many times in our lives when we are unable to endure such a meeting!

In one of my churches there was a teenage girl who was most impressionable and—shall we say—confused? One day she came into my study and asked me to accompany her to the sanctuary where I could "turn on God" for her. After a moment's confusion I realized that she was referring to the Gethsemane Window over the altar, electrified since the education unit had been constructed, obstructing the natural light. She wanted me to turn on the current so that the window would light up and she could "see" God. "Denise!" I scolded, "Even if I could 'turn on' God for you, I wouldn't because the Bible says that no one can look upon His face and live!" This theological subtlety must have eluded her, for she became indignant and threatened to go to another church where the preacher was not so "uppity." At that point I realized that there was no reasoning with her. "All right," I sighed, "Let's see if we can 'turn on' God."

Metropolitan Anthony handled a similar situation with more grace. A young man came to him and asked him to show him God. He replied that he could not, but even if he could, the man wouldn't be able to see Him because in order to meet God one must have something in common with Him. The man looked puzzled, so Metropolitan Anthony asked him if there was any passage in the Gospel that moved him particularly. The man replied that there was. "In the eighth chapter of the Gospel of John, the passage concerning the woman taken in adultery."

"Good!" the priest replied, "This is one of the most beautiful and moving passages. Now sit back and ask yourself, who are you in the scene described? Are you the Lord, or at least on His side, full of mercy, of understanding and full of faith in this woman who can repent and become a new creature? Are you one of the older men who walk out at once because they are aware of their own sins, or one of the young ones who wait?"

The man thought a few moments and replied, "No, I feel I am the only Jew who would not have walked out but would have stoned the woman!"

"Then," Metropolitan Anthony replied, "Thank God that He does not allow you to meet Him face to face."(7)

That the will of God should be fulfilled in us is the only aim and sole criterion of an attentive, living prayer. Or as Theophane the Recluse puts it:

"Ask yourself, 'Have I prayed well today?' Do not try to find out how deep your emotions were, or how much deeper you understand things divine. Ask yourself, 'Am I doing God's will better than before?' If you are, prayer has brought it fruits, if you are not, it has not, whatever amount of understanding or feeling you may have derived from the time spent in the presence of God."(8)

As we proceed through these chapters, let us never lose sight of this essential question.

(1) Leech, Kenneth, *True Prayer: An Invitation to Christian Spirituality*, Harper & Row Publishers, San Francisco, 1986, p. 52.

(2) Underhill, Evelyn, *Worship*, Crossroad Publishing Company, 370 Lexington Ave, New York, NY 10017, 1989, p. 27.

(3) Bloom, Anthony, *Living Prayer*, Templegate Publishers, Springfield, IL 62705, 1966, p. 56.

(4) *Op. Cit.*, Leech, p. 53.

(5) *Op. Cit.*, Bloom, pps. 51-52.

(6) *Bloom, Anthony. Beginning to Pray.* Paulist Press. p. 46

(7) *Op. Cit.*, pps. 27-28.

(8) *Op. Cit.*, p. 62.

THE NECESSITY OF SPIRITUAL DIRECTION

In 1980, *Soul Friend* by Kenneth Leech, appeared. This study of spiritual direction remains the pioneering work in the field and has clarified my own understanding of the discipline, and heightened my sense of its urgency for our time. He tells us that the way of Christian Perfection, or knowledge of God, cannot be begun in us apart from the discovery of the self, nor can there be any maturity apart from this discovery. (1) Any preparation to receive this knowledge requires work and spiritual training. This spiritual training involves nothing less than taking up the cross. Its purpose is the development of Christ within us by an increased cooperation with the Holy Spirit.(2)

This training, while it requires all the work we can do, is the achievement of the Holy Spirit. If it leads to wholeness, it must be a painful process, for birth itself is painful. This is what T.S. Eliot tells us in his Journey of the Magi:

"..were we led all the way for
Birth or death? There was a birth, certainly,
We had evidence and no doubt. I had seen birth and death,
But had thought they were different; this Birth was
Hard and bitter agony for us, like death, our Death."(3)

Often, it seems to me, the pastoral counseling movement sees the upset associated with this "hard and bitter agony" as a personality disorder or dysfunction. While it certainly appears dysfunctional, it may not be a problem of "adjustment," or even of self-actualization. Self-actualization is not the end of the journey to Perfection. It is hardly even a good beginning! Without the surrender that must follow, one's journey cannot begin at all. It may even be true, as Thomas Merton has said, that much pastoral counseling becomes "the instru-

23

ment for forming and preserving the mentality of the organization man."(4) The organization man or woman, I'm afraid, has a difficult time responding to the urging of the Holy Spirit.

I do not suggest that the clinical model is either wrong-headed or that it has not contributed to an enormous amount of healing. I only suggest that, as Jesus said, some demons a.k.a. disorders are only cast-out by much prayer. (Mark 9:29)

Many years ago I glanced out my office window and noticed an extremely distraught young woman in a hospital gown, making her way up the icy hill to my church. While she was yet several hundred yards away, I telephoned the hospital switchboard, because the markings on her gown identified her as a patient of its mental health facility down the hill. Only then did I let her in. She took a furtive look around, and, with slurred speech, indicated that God had led her up the hill and that I must help her. Here was an extremely disoriented woman clad only in a hospital gown, oblivious to the cold, seeking sanctuary in a cold church, and comfort from a pastor who was scared to death of her. Yet, I found myself asking, "How can I help you?"

"Oh Reverend," she pleaded, "I'm so scared. I don't know what to do!"

I looked out the window and saw the flashing lights of the ambulance. Two burly young men in white uniforms muscled their way in, followed by a solemn female nurse with a syringe. "Mary," she said in reassuring tones, "We're going to give you a shot! It'll relax you." Moments later, a relaxed Mary was strapped onto the gurney and whisked away.

I was right to call the medical people, but why hadn't I offered Mary Christ? Christ was the One she was seeking! In the days that followed, why didn't I visit Mary in her ward? I did nothing because I thought it irresponsible to interfere. She was, after all, in the hands of the professionals, and to meddle would have placed me and my congregation in an adversary relationship with an institution that, at that time, tended to regard religion as guilt-producing, and thus an impediment to the healing process.

R.D. Laing may take his criticism of the clinical model a bit too far, but it does contain an element of truth, as my own experience would indicate:

". . . if they go to a Christian priest, the priest will probably refer them to the psychiatrist, and the psychiatrist will refer them to a mental hospital, and the mental hospital will refer them to the electric shock machine. And if that is not our contemporary mode of crucifying Christ, what is?"(5)

Several years after this incident, I found myself to be "dysfunctional." I mistook what the mystics called "dryness" or "aridity" for what might be clinically described as "depression." Fortunately, I eventually found a clinical psychologist who turned out to be something of a theologian. Ironically, this was at a time when my own sermons were laced with the then-current terminology of "pop-psychology." After several sessions, he helped me to see that my problem was not an inadequate sense of self, or even low self-esteem, but my steadfast refusal to surrender the self to which I tenaciously clung and sought to affirm. In a word, he helped me to surrender that identity so that another could begin to grow in its place. He helped me to die to a whole multiplicity of selves and to begin to live from another center, my deepest self, or my God-conscious self.

This God-consciousness is the aim of spiritual direction. This God-consciousness is the beginning of that journey which brings us to the place where we can say with Paul that "it is not I who live, but Christ who lives in me." (Gal. 2:20)

The spiritual traveler must pass from self-consciousness through self-surrender to receive any degree of God-consciousness. If self-knowledge is the beginning of God-consciousness, it is truly, as Thomas Merton would have it, "the first step to sanctity."(6) If, on the other hand, self-knowledge and self-actualization is pursued for its own sake, it will lead to a dead end. If we would progress in our journey toward Christian Perfection, we must go into training, and for the journey a spiritual guide may prove helpful.

Spiritual direction was first widely practiced in the desert monastic communities of North Africa and the Sinai during the first centuries following the wholesale adoption of Christianity by the Roman Empire. Those who withdrew to find a spiritual purity no longer evident in the life of the world soon discovered that the solitary life posed great dangers without proper guidance. St. John Climacus, perhaps the most eloquent early advocate of spiritual direction, has this advice for the spiritual traveler: ". . . you have undertaken to travel by a short and rough road, along which there is one false turning, that which they call self-direction."(7)

In the same spirit, St. Basil tells his readers to find someone who may serve as a sure guide in the work of leading a holy life, and who can direct the traveler along the straight road to God. He warns that to believe that one has no need of counsel is great pride.(8) St. Simeon the New Theologian adds that "if someone observes perfect obedience towards his spiritual father, he becomes free of all cares, because once and for all he has laid all his cares on the shoulders of his spiritual father."(9) The monks Callistos and Ignatius tell us that one's spiritual father should be "as a man bearing the spirit within him; leading a humble life corresponding to his words; lofty in vision of mind; humble in thought of himself; of a good disposition in everything, and generally such as a teacher of Christ should be, according to divine words."(10)

The role of the spiritual guide or director perhaps enjoyed its greatest flowering in Russia, where it continues to the present day. There, a spiritual guide is called a staretz, which means "old man." From this we must not conclude that every staretz was and is necessarily old and male. The designation has always been an informal one, and, as always, is given to a person revered by his or her followers as one upon whom the spirit rests as the culmination of a long life of simplicity and humility. Such a guide was deemed necessary by the hermit in *The Way of a Pilgrim,* who said, "If certain of them (spiritual solitaries) have fallen into self-deception and fanaticism, that was the result of pride, of not having a director, and of taking appearance and imagination for reality."(11) Leech identifies the three principal features of such a guide: "First, he is a man of insight and discernment (diakrisis). He is able to see into the heart of another, a gift which is the fruit of ascetic struggle... Second, he is a man with the ability to love others and make the sufferings of others his own... Third, he is one with the power to transform the cosmos by the intensity of his love."(12)

The road of Christian Perfection is a dangerous one inasmuch as the traveler suffers from the danger of being blinded by pride and unbalanced either by a reliance on ecstatic feelings on the one hand and by despair on the other.(13) Because the traveler disciplines the self to receive the revelation which is nothing if not supernatural, there is always the danger of being misled, and of falling prey to delusion, for Satan appears to the credulous and the unwary as an angel of Light. (2 Cor. 11:14) Thus it becomes the essential role of the spiritual guide to judge between truth and falsehood, or to test the spirits to see if they be of God. (1 John 4:1) For St. Ignatius, identifying and confronting evil forces is the task of spiritual direction. The director's task is to uncover Satan's wiles and to safeguard his disciples from false choices.(14)

The spiritual guide, in addition to having the gift of discernment, also points the spiritual traveler to the Sacraments, the means of grace, and the goodly fellowship of believers. The capacity to give love and receive grace is the test of whether or not the journey is leading the traveler to the Father of Lights, for, as the Great Evangelist puts it:

"Anyone who claims to love God and hates his brother, is a liar. A man who does not love the brother he can see, cannot love God, whom he has not seen." (1 John 4:20)

Or to paraphrase the Apostle Paul, "He who stands without the means of grace that the Body of Christ supplies, must take heed, in case he fails." (1 Cor. 10:12)

Spiritual direction is never "client" centered, but a relationship that grows out of the mutual seeking of the guided and the guide.(15) The guided and the guide together are nourished by the divine-human relationship. The guided and the guide together are part of the vine, sustained by the branch which is Christ, who says, "Cut off from me you can do nothing." (John 15:5)

Although a mutuality of seeking unites the guided and the guide, the guide in the relationship owes the capacity to lead to the wisdom, experience and divine illumination that he or she has already received. Divine illumination, according to Augustine Baker, is the one element that separates the guide from the guided, and indeed is the most important part. He insists that "neither natural judgment, learning, nor experience altogether are absolutely sufficient to qualify a person to be a guide in the internal ways of the spirit. Often, he says, 'an actual supernatural illumination will be necessary.' "(16)

In seeking a guide, there is a type of mutuality that should be avoided, and that is mutuality of temper. Baker warns, "avoid one of like temper, for passion which blinds the seeker will also blind the director."(17) In addition, the effective guide never encourages what amounts to a dependency relationship, but must deliver the guided to the direct influence of the Holy Spirit. It was Tauler who warned that certain spiritual guides are like hunting dogs who eat the hare instead of bringing it to their master.(18)

How does one find a guide? Although Leech has suggested the formation of a network of spiritual directors, the thought of such an association (accredited by whom?) carries with it the risk of professionalism, if not elitism. Apart from the qualities enumerated above, which come from life's school, nourished by the Holy Spirit within the life of the church, such a structure may neither be advisable nor necessary.

The hermit's advice in *The Way of the Pilgrim* may prove to be the best last word:

"During the practice of inward activity of heart, a genuine and well-informed director is required. If such a one is not at hand, then you must diligently search for one. If you do not find him, then, calling contritely upon God for help, draw instruction and guidance from the teaching of the Holy Fathers and verify it from the Word of God set forth in the holy scriptures."(19) He adds:

"Here one must also take into consideration the fact that the seeker of goodwill and zeal can obtain something useful in the way of instruction from ordinary people also. For the holy Fathers assure us likewise, that if with faith and right intention one questions even a Saracen, he can speak words of value to us. If, on the other hand, one asks for instruction from a Prophet, without faith and a righteous purpose, then even he will not satisfy us."(20)

(1) Leech, Kenneth, *Soul Friend: The Practice of Christian Spirituality,* Harper & Row, Publishers, San Francisco, 1980, p. 105.

(2) *Ibid.,* p. 38.

(3) T.S. Eliot, *Collected Poems* 1909-1962, Harcourt, Brace & World, Inc., New York, 1963., p. 100.

(4) Op Cit., Leech, p. 102, cited from *An Introduction to Christian Mysticism,* Lectures given at the Abbey of Gethsemani, MS (1961), p. 145.

(5) *Ibid.,* p. 120, cited from Laing, R.D., in *The Role of Religion in Mental Health* (1967), p. 57.

(6) *Ibid.,* p. 170, as cited from Merton, Thomas, Sermon 71.

(7) Luibheid, Colm and Russell, Norman (Trans.) John Climacus: *The Ladder of Divine Ascent,* Paulist Press, New York, Ramsey, Toronto, 1982., p. 92.

(8) *Op. Cit.,* Leech, p. 41, as cited from R. Garrigou-Lagrange, *The Three Ages of Interior Life,* (1960 ed.)I, p. 256.

(9) Kadloubovsky E, and Palmer, G.E.H., *Writings from the Philokalia on Prayer of the Heart,* Faber and Faber, London-Boston, 1983, p. 155.

(10) *Ibid.*, pps. 173-4.

(11) French, R.M., (Trans.) *The Way of a Pilgrim and the Pilgrim Continues in His Way,* Crossroad Books, the Seabury Press, NY, 1965, p. 218.

(12) Op Cit., Leech, pps. 48-9.

(13) *Ibid.*, p. 184.

(14) *Ibid.*, p. 130 as cited from Exercises 17.

(15) *Ibid.*, p. 34.

(16) *Ibid.*, p. 63, cited from *Holy Wisdom,* I.2.2., para. 11.

(17) *Ibid.*, p. 63, same, I.2.2., para. 13.

(18) *Ibid.*, p. 56.

(19) *Op. Cit.,* French, pps. 220-1.

(20) *Ibid.*, p. 221.

INDIVIDUAL PRAYER

THE MYSTIC WAY

True prayer begins with God who moves our spirit, as the Gospel song tells us, to seek Him seeking us. To believe that we who pray take the initiative is a conceit born of pride! The impulse to pray always begins with God. We may either choose to obey or ignore that impulse, but the impulse itself always begins with God. Through our prayers He reveals that His will is wholly Love, and that our response to that will must be love as well. Even our love for God draws its energy from the source of Love itself, which is God.

This Love cannot be mediated through knowledge, but must be revealed to love. It is not reasonable to forgive infinitely, as our Savior demands. Knowledge can never produce the will to forgive but Love working within us can and does. Our life, unless it be transformed by this Love, will never produce the fruits of Love. The person who continually prays finds his or her life transformed from one of "knowing" to one of believing, and from one ruled by the many selves to one lived according to God's will, which is Love.

Yet the self—the deepest self—is the clay from which God may fashion a vessel for His love. The person who prays discovers that the deepest self is the clay which must be shaped, molded and fired by Love. This God-created entity is what Christian tradition calls the soul.

The starting point for prayer is to place the self in the hands of God. This process, whether long or short, is an arduous one, which the mystics call purgation. This is the clay's surrender to the potter, the surrender of the vanquished to the conqueror as yet unseen, and the lover's surrender to the beloved hidden behind the veil.

This yielding may begin hesitatingly, reluctantly, and with apprehension, but over time these misgivings must give way to the joy of that new awareness that comes of spiritual rebirth.

Our initial apprehension, though understandable, is nevertheless misplaced. Edgar Jackson assures us that while prayer uses the self, it only uses that self that is willing to be used. Prayer does not overpower, but invites. It makes an overture.(1)

Some time ago, old friends stopped by for lunch, but it was soon apparent that the reunion was going to be difficult. It seemed, during the course of the conversation, that my wife and I were doing all the listening. Not once in the four-hour visit did this couple direct a single question towards us, although there was much to inquire about. Since we had last seen our friends we had raised our family, and buried loved ones.

A week after the visit, we received a note which read, "We're praying for you because we sense that you are deeply troubled." Deeply troubled? Yes, but mostly by their insensitivity and self-absorption during the visit! Then it occurred to us that we were the victims of a ploy which years earlier would have had us eating out of their hands. But the relationship—if it was to continue—needed to be placed on a new footing, outside their control.

The frightening thing about a relationship is that the more we need it, the more we must yield to it. If the possibility of prayer fills us with apprehension, it may be precisely because in prayer, we find we must yield to the Other who is Love.

Our yielding, however, leads us to that new level of awareness that the mystics call illumination. Within this stage we begin to see our passions as subject to the will of the One who is Love, and not to those separate selves we still permit to control us.

Now and then the television talk-shows bring to light some person who claims to have multiple personalities. Actually, every child of God, self-conscious or not, is composed of a multiplicity of selves, each of which may be wedded to one or more of the passions. While some of these selves may be relatively benign, others may tend toward yielding to demonic powers. There is an old story about the preacher whose eulogy for "Uncle Charles" was so moving that the mourners peered a second time into the coffin to see whether or not they had wandered into the wrong chapel! The preacher, however, had not misrepresented "Uncle Charles." He had eulogized the only self that the deceased had revealed to him.

Prayer would gather the multiplicity of our straying selves into that single fold which is the deepest self, or the God-directed self.

Thus, the fearful selves are brought under the influence of the faithful self, or as Edgar Jackson puts it:

"Fear with its disorganizing effect upon life can create a downward spiral of apprehension, and suspicion of self and others. The fear-dominated life is filled with gruesome experience. The mood and attitude of faith can change the same external experience into an entirely different internal response. What has been feared can be accepted with confidence. The act of praying for sustaining faith can take the Gardens of Gethsemane and turn them into the triumphs of Easter."(2)

As we move through prayer away from an attitude of fear toward the multiplicity of selves within and toward mastery over them, we find that we also begin to regard our external enemies with compassion rather than fear. During the 1991 Persian Gulf War, we prayed for Saddam Hussein rather than fantasize about what harm we might inflict upon him, had we the chance. Through prayer we discover that feelings of hatred are ultimately self-defeating and self-destroying. During the process of illumination which is prayer, this hate-filled self, or the "Saddam Hussein" self gradually comes under the influence of the deepest self.

The mystics speak of the ultimate aim of prayer as Union with God. This impulse to Union is described by St. Augustine as that restlessness which remains until it finds its rest in God. Prayer, if it is to approach Union with this God, must move toward that fulfillment of the deepest self which is entire self-transcendence. This is Love beckoning to love in a way that knowledge can neither define nor comprehend. Indeed, if we would wait for knowledge to interpret this Love, we would never move at all. Jackson says in this regard:

"I do not need to know how to breathe before I take a breath. I do not need to know why I eat before I nourish my body. If we were always to wait upon explanations, we should die before we had the answers."(3)

The more prayer enables the self to transcend itself, the more attuned we become to the deepest self or the God-self. When this process is completed in the resurrection we shall, as Paul says, know, even as we are known.

When I repeat the Apostles' Creed, I sometimes wish that it could be rewritten to read, "I believe in God the Father Almighty, and God the Father Almighty believes in me." It is precisely because God believes in us that He has given us the capacity for self-transcendence. That capacity accounts for the restlessness within and for the impulse that would prod each child of God toward that Union for which we were made. Prayer moves us ever toward the possibility of that Union, and thereby our multiplicity of straying selves is gradually gathered into the fold of the deepest self, which increasingly becomes an instrument of His peace.

PURGATION

Once I was informed that a parishioner was staying away from services because of something I had said in a sermon. This man had been a thorn in my side since my first days in that parish and I found myself going to his home to see if we could be reconciled. When, in the course of that visit, it became apparent that no reconciliation was going to take place, I suggested that we might pray together that the enmity between us might be lifted, "You can pray all you like, Reverend," he replied, "but it isn't going to make any difference."

Now I realize something that I suspect he began to sense even as the visit was taking place: I was not there to reconcile at all, but to make some sort of point. He perceived my visit as a kind of spiritual one-upsmanship, and he would have none of it! The 'point,' I now concede, was his. Unless prayer is a purging, or cleansing of the will, that prayer "isn't going to make any difference." Before we are to make any progress in the way that leads to Christian Perfection, or Union with God, the self must be purged utterly of self-will, self-love, and the will to power. Meister Eckhart has said so succinctly: "..what God wills is that we should give up willing."(4) God may give us tongues of men and angels. He may even give us visions of light, but He will never give us Himself until we give up self altogether.(5) We may claim to believe in God, and even to love God, but unless we submit our wills to His, and desire in all things to please Him, we will be of no more use to His Kingdom than the rich young ruler.

Faith lives, moves and has its being in the works that it does. These works cannot reflect the love of God unless faith sacrifices all things to which self-will is attached. The greatest work faith can do is struggle to put God's will above self-will. Otherwise, it will amount to nothing. We know that we are at last in conformity with God's will when, as St. Thomas Aquinas has said, there remain no obstacles to

36

prevent us from loving God with all our being.(6) Submission and faith must go hand in hand. "Only in the submission which is faith," says Thomas Merton, "can we 'know' God and find in that knowledge true peace."(7)

Many, however, who find themselves drawn to Christ, cannot bear to hear the call to surrender, and like the rich young ruler, must go away sorrowful. St. Teresa of Avila gave this advice to her Carmelite sisters:

"...if when he tells us what we must do in order to be perfect, we turn our backs upon him and go away sorrowfully, what do you expect His Majesty to do, for the reward which he is to give us must of necessity be proportionate with the love which we bear to him?"(8)

If ever we are to walk with Christ, ours must be an Apostleship of surrender. Judas heard this call, surrendered for a time, and for a time enjoyed communion with his Lord. But Judas' surrender was not continuous, and because of this, he found himself lost. Unless our surrender is continuous, we will surely also find ourselves lost, as Judas did.(9)

For St. Teresa, the way of continuous surrender is exemplified by Mary Magdalene, who became a saint, not because she thought much, but because she loved much, and did whatever aroused this love.(10) A spark of this love must be there before we can even speak of surrender. A surrender that is coerced may cause one to be obedient for a time, but unless this surrender be tempered by love, it can come to no good end. Surrender to another without love is a type of Hell. The resentment it engenders, and its consequence, may even drive one mad.

For several years I took communion to an elderly lady who always refused it. Her humble kitchen table was piled high with trinkets she had received from the various televangelists, and solicitation letters which, if answered, would keep the trinkets coming. She knew that I disapproved and would always gesture in the direction of this stuff and say in her gentle yet defiant tone, "I help 'em all!" One day when I asked her why she wouldn't take communion, she replied, "The fact is, I'm unworthy, and one who partakes unworthily partakes of damnation!"

When I asked her why she thought herself unworthy, her eyes moistened and she spoke of her childhood, and of the little sister she was expected to raise after her father had been stricken with tuberculosis. So bitterly did she resent this responsibility that she wished the child dead. Her bitterness remained undiminished even when the little sister herself came down with the disease, and eventually died. "So you see," the old woman said, "I got my wish! Now do you see why I shan't take communion?"

I told her about Mary Magdalene—a very bad woman indeed—whom the Lord loved. I described how, every time she thought of Him and how her sins had been forgiven and forgotten, she loved Him all the more. But this lady would have none if it! "Young man," she responded, "every day for eighty years I have seen a vision of that helpless little face. It's the Lord's punishment for wishing my little sister dead. So I shan't take communion! It wouldn't be right!" There was no convincing her. There was no consolation that she would accept. She took that awful burden to her grave!

The surrender of the will must be accompanied by the letting-go of our sins, real or imagined. Until we begin to do this, it cannot be said that we have truly surrendered!

The author of *The Cloud of Unknowing* gives us an insight about our need to surrender our sins as exemplified by Mary Magdalene:

"Did she come down from the heights of her desire to the depths of her sinful life, and search about in the foul malodorous bog and dunghill of her sins, dragging them up one by one with all of their circumstances, and sorrowing and weeping on each of them? No indeed, she did nothing of the sort. And why? Because God made her understand, by the grace within her soul, that she could never achieve anything thus. She was more likely by these means to raise up in herself a tendency to sin again, rather than to obtain by such methods a true forgiveness of her sins."(11)

We may find, like Magdalene herself, that once we have put our sins behind us—surrendered them with our self-will—that we may find ourselves so consumed by love for Christ that we will no longer pay any attention to whether we were ever a sinner or not.(12) This surrender, if it be authentic, is for pure joy. Not to surrender, in these circumstances, would be a denial of our deepest self.

Before there can be joy, however, there must be the will to believe. This will to believe must accompany the surrender of the will itself. Each step of our walk with Christ requires a further surrender of the will. Faith demands this before Christ will reveal Himself further.

When our surrender ceases, so does the possibility of this revelation. As Thomas Merton tells us, none of this is ever easy:

"Christian contemplation is precipitated by crisis within crisis and anguish within anguish. It is born of spiritual conflict. It is a victory that suddenly appears in the hour of defeat. It is the providential solution of problems that seem to have no solution. It is the reconciliation of enemies that seem to be irreconcilable. It is a vision in which love, mounting into the darkness which no reason can penetrate unites in one bond all the loose strands that intelligence alone cannot connect together, and with this cord draws the whole being of man into Divine Union, the effects of which will some day overflow into the world outside him."(13)

It remains for us to surrender to Him, and this process begins when we meet Him in prayer.

ILLUMINATION

"Modern psychology," writes George Maloney, "has given us the phrase 'meaningful relationship.' "(14) For many it means "that which meets my need for pleasure." A relationship of this type, if it can be called a relationship at all, cannot grow beyond the fantasy world that hedges it about. When this same attitude finds expression in the worship life of the church, it will be overheard saying, "Now that was a meaningful 'worship' experience!" While this may mean, "Now that addressed my life!" it is more likely to mean, "Now that was a pleasant experience!"

The Christian life, once it has passed beyond the stage of mere spiritual self-gratification, must undergo a thorough purging of the will which has also been called the annihilation of the ego. Paul calls it a putting away of childish things. (I Cor. 13:12) Far from being the end of the journey, this is the place where our faith either begins to mature or it dies altogether. Now we see through a glass darkly and we have arrived at that second stage of the journey the mystics call illumination. This stage may be even more of a trial than the purgation of the will, for the process of illumination requires nothing less than a liberation from the passions. This is not a work that is within our power to accomplish. As Meister Eckhart has said: "God must do it, and you must undergo it."(15)

Until one arrives at this place, knowledge is acquired primarily through the media of the senses. This, however, is a birth from within, which reverses the process of knowing and causes one to move beyond "knowing" to "unknowing."(16) At one time, images, words and the "props of sensible consolation"(17) served to guide us. These, however, were ideas about God and not God Himself. Now everything we knew, or thought we knew, is of little use, for we stand facing a wall that our poor intellectual powers will never penetrate.

Many never get beyond this wall, turning back to the sensible consolations which once gave them comfort. But these do so no longer. They have grown empty, sterile and cold. Those who surrender these consolations, rather than surrender to them, are few. But the few who do are given entrance to that twilight of the passions before the dark night of the soul. For those who arrive at this place, Meister Eckhart offers these words:

"...by keeping yourself empty and bare, merely tracking and following and giving up yourself to this darkness and ignorance without turning back, you may well win that which is all things. And the more you are barren of yourself and ignorant of all things, the nearer you are thereto."(18)

Illumination cannot be accomplished by the Holy Spirit until we surrender the passions. For as Isaac the Syrian has said:

"Until the outer man dies to the whole world, not only to sin, but also to every activity, and equally, until the inner man dies to evil thoughts and the natural stirrings of the body weaken..until then the sweetness of the Divine Spirit will not rise in a man..Divine thoughts will not enter his soul and will remain unsensed and not seen. And until in his heart a man has made passive the cares of this life, and entrusts this care to God, spiritual ecstasy will not spring forth in him."(19)

The protest many of our Age make in the face of such a challenge is that we are only human, and the passions are not to be denied. The Age counsels that it would be better if we accepted the passions as part of our nature, and that yielding to them now and again is healthier than suppressing them altogether. It is true that to resist the passions for no other object than to suppress them is probably pointless, dangerous and stupid! If, however, our object is that state where illumination becomes possible, the benefits will be incalculable, for as Thomas

Merton has said: "...life is far too great a gift to be squandered on anything less than perfection."(20)

Without this yearning for Christian Perfection, the disciplines of contemplation, which are recollection, meditation, prayer, mortification of the desires and some measure of solitude, will only serve to make us miserable. In fact, when that "evil spirit" which we have cast-out by the strength of our own will returns of its own accord and finds its house unoccupied, swept and tidied, it will surely collect seven others, more evil than itself, and we will find ourselves worse-off than we were before. (Matt. 12:43-45) Our liberation from the passions must be the work of God, who looks upon us in mercy and makes us what we desire to be.

Yet, even after this is accomplished, the divide between the Created and the Creator remains, though now it may appear as darkness and a cloud rather than an impenetrable wall. Now, says Paul, we know, but only in part. The face of God may be seen through the gloom, but obscurely. The nearer our approach, the blacker the darkness and the deeper the obscurity. As St. John of the Cross has said:

"...just as the nearer a man approaches the sun, the greater are the darkness and the affliction caused him through the great splendor of the sun, and through the weakness and impurity of the eyes. In the same way, so immense is the spiritual light of God, and so greatly does it transcend our natural understanding, that the nearer we approach it, the more it blinds and darkens us..."(21)

As the passions fall away, however, this darkness becomes our friend. So, the author of The Cloud of Unknowing advises us, we may set ourselves to rest in this darkness, crying to Him whom we love. If ever we are to see Him or experience Him at all, it must be in this cloud and in this darkness.(22) As our eyes become accustomed to the gloom, we find the capacity to receive unshakable joy. If this is darkness, it is a bright and shining darkness, of which the Psalmist spoke when he said: "...the night is as bright as the day..." (Psalm 139:12)

With this joy come two gifts or capacities which are called detachment and discernment.(23) These every mature Christian has received in some measure, and their presence cannot be mistaken!

Detachment is that passionlessness many mistake for apathy, but it is nothing of the sort! Instead, it is that "passionate passionlessness" which loves nothing in all the world more than the knowledge of

God.(24) When our Lord was on His way to Jerusalem and Mary sat at his feet while her sister Martha fumed, he advised Martha that her sister had chosen the one thing necessary. Meister Eckhart tells us that this the same as saying that one who would be serene and pure needs this one thing—detachment.(25) Mary loved her Lord more than any created thing, and this defined and vivified all her other loves. Thus, detachment puts everything in its proper perspective. It renounces and rejects any pleasure that presents itself to the senses, if it is not for the honor and glory of God.(26)

Once our spirit is darkened to attachments, the capacity for discernment makes itself known. As our Lord said, "When your eye is sound, your whole body is filled with light." (Luke 11:34) At one time our spirit tried to satisfy its yearnings for God with fabrications and illusions, and frequently lapsed into blindness, the fruits of which are restlessness and inordinate desire. Now, however, the eye is clear inasmuch as faith, hope and love have been focused through the influence of the Holy Spirit. Intelligence and reason still inform us as before, but now they have been pressed into the service of faith. In a compelling image, Thomas Merton likens intelligence and reason to the lights of an automobile on a dark highway. "The only way a driver can keep to the road is by using his headlights (for the) way of faith is necessarily obscure.. Nevertheless, our reason penetrates the darkness enough to show us the light of the road ahead.."(27) What is it in this dark night that propels the engine but the "passionate passionlessness" of the Spirit? Being in darkness, our spirit "feels itself without God and without Him and dying for love of Him."(28)

Mary Magdalene is an appropriate model for this night journey, for such was the inebriating power and boldness of this love that even though she knew that her Beloved was sealed inside the sepulchre and surrounded by a company of soldiers, she allowed none of these to restrain her, but journeyed by night with her ointments of devotion.(29)

It is this devotion that puts all our other loves in order. The "meaningful relationship," which is longed-for for its own sake, will never effect the transformation of our being that faith's awakening accomplishes during that dark night. It is through this illumination that we are "saved." Through it we are born anew. Thus we begin to live that life of which Paul speaks—a life that is not our own, but Christ, living in us. (Gal. 3:20)

42

UNION

Every creature which lives according to its nature fulfills the will of its Creator. Yet humankind, when it fulfills its own nature, rarely rises above the level of beasts, for it is created in the image and likeness of God. It is God's intention that each of His children stretch every nerve and sinew toward the source of his or her being. Each of His children is endowed with an infinite capacity for union with Him in grace, if not in nature.

Each self-conscious child of God has already experienced, in the deepest self, the dark flame of desire for this Union. As each man or woman receives the Word of God by faith, that flame burns with an ever darker intensity.(30) Thus it is that the deepest self, the God-self, rises above the world, the flesh and the devil to that frontier of seeing what no eye may see nor ear may hear. This is the threshold of Union where God may reveal some of the secret things He has prepared for those who love Him.

At this threshold of the door to eternity which stands open within, we watch and wait. We watch and wait at the frontier of a bright abyss—so bright that it seems dark to us. At this threshold we burn with the desire to see the fullness of the Light and cry out to God as Moses did in Sinai's cloud, "Show me your face!"

It is by surrender alone that we arrive at this frontier, and here we must wait. God cannot give Himself to us until we give ourselves to Him, but the times and seasons are His to determine. Therefore, we must wait, and as we wait, it may be His will to "...send out a ray of spiritual light, piercing (the) cloud of unknowing between you and him, (to) show you some of his secrets, of which man may not, or cannot speak."(32)

What is this surrender? What is this perfect receptivity which prepares us to receive this ray of spiritual light which will permit us, as Paul says, to know Him even as we are known? Three things constitute this perfect receptivity. The deepest self must be dead to itself; it must have the capacity to stand outside itself, or be detached from itself; and it must be becoming so transformed in the will of God that its only happiness is God and God alone.(33)

What does it mean to say that the deepest self must be dead to itself? Meister Eckhart gives us the answer:

"What must a man be to see God? He must be dead. 'No man can see me and live,' said the Lord. Now St. Gregory says, 'that man is dead who is dead to the world.' By dying to the world we do not die to God."(34)

Although this same truth is enshrined in the traditions of the Revival movement, we may have assumed that this is part of a charming albeit naive faith that we have outgrown. It well may be, however, that we are the ones who are "charming" and "naive"! When our ancestors sang:

"Fill me now, fill me now,
Jesus, come and fill me now;
Fill me with Thy Hallowed Presence,
Come, O come and fill me now."(35)

they knew that God could not fill them with His presence until they would undergo an immolation of the self. This receptivity was the fruit of a devotion and a determination that we may never approach. Until we do, however, we will not "see" God.

How can we know, assuming that we would be dead to the world, that we have approached the threshold of this receptivity? We will know, as St. Nilus has said, when everything earthly has the "semblance of ashes and dung."(36)

Then we will begin to approach the peace that passes understanding. Until the veil of the passions is lifted from the eyes of the mind, we cannot be filled with awe.(37)

The deepest self must have the capacity to stand outside itself, or be detached from itself. Paul, describing his own vision of this peace, speaks with this detachment:

"I know a Christian man who fourteen years ago (whether in the body or out of it, I do not know—God knows) was caught up as far as the third heaven. And I know that this same man (whether in the body or out of it, I do not know—God knows) was caught up into paradise, and heard words so secret that human lips may not repeat them.." (2 Cor. 12:2-4 NEB)

In recent years, Elizabeth Kubler-Ross and others have attempted to make these "out-of-body" experiences the subject of scientific enquiry, for such is the arrogance of the human spirit. Natural knowledge will never penetrate the mysteries of God, any more, says Thomas Merton, "than a flashlight can help an owl to find its way about when it is dazzled by the light of high noon."(38)

44

Here below, these glimpses over the threshold are never more than fleeting. The disciples are never permitted to stay atop the Mount of Transfiguration for long, but must return to the valley of human need. As St. Nilus has said: "If God did not place a limit to such a state how long would one not dwell in it! And if it were permitted to last throughout a man's life, he would never wish to turn away from this wondrous vision."(39)

The deepest self must be becoming so transformed in the will of God that its only happiness is God and God alone. Once flooded with this joy, we become united with God in grace. There is then no division between the self and God, both here below and in the happiness of heaven. But, as the author of The Cloud of Unknowing emphasizes, "though you are with him in grace you are yet far, far beneath him in nature."(40)

This joy is the "bond of perfectness" so dear to the Wesleys. It approaches the Beatific Vision of St. Teresa and the abandonment of the soul to the Beloved, lauded by St. John of the Cross. It is the ray of spiritual light, described by the author of *The Cloud of Unknowing.* It is also the resurrection faith, described by Teresa when she said: "He will come into the center of the soul without using a door, as He did when He came to His disciples and said, 'Peace be with you!' and when He left the sepulchre without removing a stone."(41) When this joy overflows within, we take no notice of anything, not even the holiest of creatures. This is why St. John of the Cross believed that Mary Magdalene did not even notice the angels at the tomb.(42)

Each self-conscious child of God has already experienced a glimmer of the dark flame of desire for God. By surrender and dying daily, we arrive at the frontier of that abyss of Light where God dwells in His fullness. It was our love for God that first caused us to surrender to Him in faith, and that same love now causes us to seek Him in an ever greater love.

May He come mysteriously to the center of your deepest self, without using a door, as He left the sepulchre without moving a stone. May His Word to you be the same "Peace" with which He greeted His disciples. May your upper room within be readied and prepared, and may He fill it with the peace that passes understanding.

(1) Jackson, Edgar N., *Understanding Prayer: An Exploration of the Nature, Disciplines, and Growth of the Spiritual Life,* Harper and Row Publishers, San Francisco, 1968, Harper and Row Paperback Edition, 1982, p. 100.

(2) *Ibid.,* pps. 103-4.

(3) *Ibid.,* p. 111.

(4) Fleming, Ursula, (Ed.), *Meister Eckhart: The Man From Whom God Nothing Hid,* Templegate Publishers, Springfield IL, 1990, p. 32, (pps. 15-16, Book 2).

(5) *Ibid.,* p. 141, (p. 185, Book 2).

(6) Merton, Thomas, *The Ascent to Truth,* a Harvest/HBJ Book, Harcourt Brace Jovanovich, Publishers, San Diego, New York, London, 1979, p. 156.

(7) *Ibid.,* p. 105.

(8) Peers, Allison E. (Ed.), *Interior Castle: St. Teresa Of Avila,* an Image Book, Doubleday, NY, a division of Bantam Doubleday Dell Publishing Group, Inc., 666 Fifth Ave., New York., NY, 10103, 1989, pps. 60-61.

(9) *Ibid.,* p. 112.

(10) *Ibid.,* p. 76.

(11) Walsh, James S.J. (Ed.), *The Cloud of Unknowing,* Paulist Press, New York, Ramsey, Toronto, 1981, p. 155.

(12) *Ibid.,* p. 155.

(13) *Op. Cit.,* Merton, pps. 107-8.

(14) Maloney, George S.J., *The Prayer of the Heart,* Ave Maria Press, Notre Dame, IN, 1981, p. 71.

(15) *Op. Cit.,* Fleming, p. 42.

(16) *Ibid.,* p. 38.

(17) *Op. Cit.,* Maloney, p. 74.

(18) *Op. Cit.,* Fleming, pps. 46-47.

(19) *Op. Cit.,* Maloney, p. 70.

(20) *Op. Cit.,* Merton, p. 10.

(21) Peers, Allison E. (Ed.), *Dark Night of the Soul* by St. John of the Cross, published by Doubleday NY, a division of Bantam, Doubleday Dell Publishing Group, Inc., 666 Fifth Ave., New York., NY, 1959, pps. 155-6.

(22) *Op. Cit.,* Walsh, pps. 120-1.

(23) *Op. Cit.,* Merton, p. 23.

(24) *Op. Cit.,* Maloney, p. 62.

(25) *Op. Cit.,* Fleming, p. 145.

(26) *Op. Cit.,* Merton, p. 55.

(27) *Ibid.,* p. 155.

(28) *Op. Cit.,* Peers, *Dark Night of the Soul,* p. 144.

(29) *Ibid.,* pps. 142-3.

(30) *Op. Cit.*, Merton, p. 315.

(31) *Ibid.*, p. 12.

(32) *Op. Cit.*, Walsh, pps. 173-4.

(33) *Op. Cit.*, Fleming, p. 64.

(34) *Ibid.*, p. 141.

(35) *Tabernacle Hymns #3*, Tabernacle Publishing Company, Corner Lake St. and Waller Ave., Chicago IL, 1967, #63, by Stokes, E.R., Copyright 1907, Hope Publishing Company.

(36) Fedotov, G.P. (Ed)., *A Treasury of Russian Spirituality*, Sheed & Ward Ltd., 1950, p. 104.

(37) *Ibid.*, p. 104.

(38) *Op. Cit.*, Merton, p. 263.

(39) *Op. Cit.*, Fedotov, p. 105.

(40) *Op. Cit.*, Walsh, p. 250.

(41) *Op. Cit.*, Peers, *Interior Castle*, p. 103.

(42) *Op. Cit.*, Peers, *The Dark Night of the Soul*, p. 168.

THE JESUS PRAYER

"Seeing the crowds, he went up on the mountain, and when he sat down his disciples came to him. And he opened his mouth and taught them..." (Matt. 5:1-2)

When I was nineteen I worked as a dishwasher in a National Park. It was a job I did not particularly like. The hours were long and the hotel kept its employees on an extremely tight leash. The scenery, however, was so magnificent that it somewhat compensated for the drudgery. The most spectacular aspect of the panorama was Mt. Wilbur, whose serene grandeur seemed to beckon and call. The hotel forbade its employees to wander from the authorized trails which only made the mountain more enticing.

On the morning of the climb, the air was fresh and invigorating. The clouds, which usually shrouded the summit, hung high in the sky, and revealed the mountain in all its naked grandeur. But the climb ended in tragedy. We lacked experience, a guide, and the proper equipment, and one of us did not return.

The Hebrews were warned not to touch the holy mountain, lest they die, and Moses ascended alone. The lofty heights of spiritual perfection were as yet forbidden to the children of Israel, and would remain veiled until Jesus invited the disciples to ascend the mountain with Him. The panorama of the heavenly vision was not to be denied them! On the mountain Jesus shared His vision of perfect love. The Beatitudes are but aspects of this perfect vision. He challenged them to claim the promise that the Beatitudes afford, and would have us also claim the promise of their fulfillment in us!

Our Lord knows our reluctance to ascend the holy mountain inasmuch as we may have begun the ascent many times, only to falter from exhaustion and turn back in despair. Although we know that if we were to approach the heights of Christian Perfection, we would be transformed in the approach, the journey is simply too arduous for us to continue on our own strength. If we are to make any progress in the way, it must be because of the grace of God working in us. As Hesychius of Jerusalem said so long ago: "It is love which elevates us—we should notice the part played by divine love in our transformation—and makes us higher than the angels."(1)

Well might we ask, "Will I be made perfect in this life?" or, "How will I know when I have arrived at the summit?" These questions may reveal that we do not yet know what lies in store for us:

"The struggler always acts himself through the help of God, but the experience of the first days makes him realize that in spite of all his efforts, if anything good is done, it is done only because he is given force from above to do it; the further he goes, the more this conviction grows and becomes deeply rooted."(2)

Yet, paradoxically, to reach the summit of Christian Perfection requires all the effort that we can make. This we learn from St. Paul, who tells us that the Christian life is like an athletic contest for which we must go into training. Nicodemus of the Holy Mountain says:

"No, no rest is allowed here. Prepare yourself for continual labor, struggle and effort, allowing for no thought of alleviation, in imitation of St. Paul who says of himself: 'I therefore so run—I follow after, if that I may apprehend—I press toward the mark' " (I Cor. 9:26; Phil. 3:12-14).(3)

The goal of the spiritual disciplines is union with the Father through contemplation in love. The Creation narratives tell us that we were created for this and from this we have fallen. Our wills, as a consequence, are held in bondage to this world and this world's goods. The spiritual disciplines would return our mind and will to their proper place that we may receive the illumination of divine grace in full measure.(4) Our Lord has told us that it is only the pure in heart who will see God. Therefore, if we are to make any progress in the ascent, we must attain purity of heart. To this end we must gird ourselves with four resolves: to never rely on ourselves in anything; to bear always in our hearts an all-daring and perfect trust in God; to struggle without ceasing; and to remain constantly in prayer.(5)

From ancient times, the prayer chosen by many who would make the ascent to Perfection has been this: "Lord Jesus Christ, Son of God, have mercy on me, a sinner." This is the discipline of the Jesus Prayer, and it combines two prayers from the Gospels: the first is the plaintive

50

cry of the two blind men, "Son of David, have mercy upon us!" (Matt. 9:27); and the muted request of the publican in the Temple, "God, have mercy on me, a sinner." (Luke 18:13) The element that these two prayers share is "have mercy."(6)

Beginners find that the Jesus Prayer, when used during times of sudden temptation, is a source of unexpected clarity and power. In time, many are drawn habitually to repeat the prayer over and over until the repetition becomes almost automatic. Eventually, the prayer becomes identified with the deepest self, and becomes automatic, like the beating of the heart. Thus is fulfilled Paul's admonition to the Thessalonians that we pray without ceasing. (I:5:17)

We must, however, be called to the Jesus Prayer as a spiritual discipline. Lev Gillet tells us:

"We must not come to the invocation of the Name through some whim or arbitrary decision on our own. We must be called to it, led to it by God. If we try to use the invocation of the Name as our main spiritual method, this choice ought to be made out of obedience to a very special vocation."(7)

We might be warned as well not to embark on our ascent alone, for, as the ancient Fathers remind us, many fall into self-delusion and even mental derangement.(8) Many find crucial support from a spiritual director or guide. Barring this, the guidance and support of a prayer fellowship is helpful. Although we must be called to the Jesus Prayer and proceed with it under the guidance of the Holy Spirit, the support of others is necessary. Paul admonished the Galatians to bear one another's burdens, so as to fulfill the law of Christ. (6:2)

If the Beatitudes are the summit of perfect love, we cannot approach our destination without grace and the spiritual discipline we provide. Grace is not merely faith, but active prayer which comes from the Holy Spirit through love.

Were it not in the mind of Christ that we should ascend to the summit of Christian Perfection and claim the promise contained in the Beatitudes, He would not have revealed His vision of perfect love to the disciples.

If we are called to the ascent with the Jesus Prayer as our helper, let us never lose sight of the publican and the two blind men. Let us remember that their prayer must be on our lips to the very end of our journey.

"Blessed are the poor in spirit, for theirs is the kingdom of heaven." (Matt. 5:3)

Before our journey toward Christian Perfection can begin, we must become aware of our fundamental destitution on the one hand, and our surfeit of riches on the other. The Jesus Prayer, with its two-fold movement, reveals our great wealth in the soaring ascent of the first part: "Lord Jesus Christ, Son of God.." The second part: "have mercy on me," causes us to return to our poverty-stricken self.(9) These two realities we must keep in balance lest we become self-assured on the one hand, and despondent on the other. St. John Chrysostom says of one who would make progress in the ascent: "He knows himself best who thinks that he is nothing: and nothing pleases God more than counting oneself last of all."(10)

Let us see the publican who prayed in the Temple as a model for our prayer life. He stood afar off saying, "God, be merciful...God be generous to me, a sinner." Evelyn Underhill tells us that it was this publican's sense of need and imperfection which was the one thing needful to make instant contact with the source of all perfection. "We need not suppose," she observes, "that he was a specially wicked man; but he knew he was an imperfect, dependent, needy man, without any claims or rights. He was a realist."(11)

What gives us that sense of proportion—-that sense of realism— which enables us to pray as we ought? St. Isaac the Syrian believes that the gift of prayer "is usually preceded by special sufferings and upheavals of the soul which lead our spirit down to the depth of the realization of its poverty and nothingness."(12) Despair alone, how-ever, can never lift us to God unless in the midst of despair we approach prayer with the simple acceptance of the divine will. It is only as we desire that the divine will be done in us that we begin our slow climb to the summit of Christian Perfection. We may, however, need to realize our poverty before we begin to discover that we are rich!

The petition, "have mercy on me, a sinner," informs us that we possess nothing we can keep. Metropolitan Anthony says:

"...it is the discovery that I am nothing and that I have nothing— total, irremediable, hopeless poverty...we do not possess life in such a way that it is impossible for anyone to take it away from us...We have a body—it will die. We have a mind—yet it is enough for one minute vessel to burst in a brain for the greatest mind to be suddenly extin-guished..."(13)

Yet, we are rich beyond accounting:

"...everything we possess is a gift and a sign of the love of God and the love of men, it is a continuous gift of divine love; and as long as we possess nothing divine love is manifested continuously and fully...it is only those who give everything away who become aware of true, total, final, irremediable, spiritual poverty, and who possess the love of God expressed in all His gifts."(14) It is as we remember all these things that we are able to pray, "Lord Jesus Christ, Son of God, have mercy on me, a sinner."

Those of us who lived near the Three Mile Island Nuclear Power Station in Central Pennsylvania will never forget the mounting dread as the full extent of the accident became known. Our family in the Midwest telephoned their pleas that we get out. Many of our neighbors did just that, and by the week-end, ours was the only light on the block. I remember walking aimlessly through deserted streets with these questions turning-over in my mind: Where could we go? If we were evacuated, how long would we be gone? If we were not allowed to return—ever—where would we be resettled? I watched the birds winging their way down the Susquehanna River, unaware that the wind beneath their wings was probably lethal. As I approached the front walk, I noticed that the front lawn was due to be mowed, but suddenly that didn't matter much. I noticed again that the paint was peeling from the window sills, a fact that distressed me earlier in the week but now proved of no consequence. The hundred silly irritations which had filled my life till that moment I could no longer summon to distract me. Suddenly none of that mattered. Only God mattered, and I saw my life with utter clarity.

Kenneth Leech tells us that "...the facing of the reality of death in daily life is central to New Testament spirituality: He who seeks to save his life will lose it. It has been said that the best way to live is to die every night..."(15)

St. John Climacus links the remembrance of death to the Jesus Prayer as he tells his monks: "Let the remembrance of death and the concise Jesus Prayer go to sleep with you and get up with you..."(16)

I am not certain that many of us get beyond equating the remembrance of death with morbidity, especially when we are young. In my first parish I often took Holy Communion to an elderly widower who had been a section foreman with the Pennsylvania Railroad. The most prominent object in his living room was a framed photograph of his

53

crew. The style of the frame indicated that the picture must have hung over his sofa for at least a half-century. As it was the only object in the room not covered with dust, it appeared that he was giving it regular attention. One day I noticed that someone had taken a crayon and marked X over nearly every head in the photograph. One day I almost blurted out, "Say, what do all these X's mean?" but his baleful glance cut me off in mid-sentence. Then I noticed that three fresh X's had appeared since my last visit. Only one face in the picture remained unmarked, and it was that of a young man whose features closely resembled his own.

I do not know to this day whether or not he was a man of deep faith, for we never talked "religion." Consequently, I do not know whether he suffered from morbidity, or possessed the gift of clarity.

The first Beatitude has two parts. The first part reminds us of our helplessness apart from faith in the Resurrection. The second reminds the believer that the blessings of heaven await the one who has acquired complete trust in God. Metropolitan Anthony says:

"...the moment you reach rock-bottom, the moment you are aware of your utter dispossession of all things, then you are on the fringe of the kingdom of God, you are aware that God is love and that He is upholding you by His love. And at that point you can pray out of your utter misery, dereliction and poverty, and you can rejoice that you are so rich with the love of God."(17)

To be poor in spirit is to be detached from everything that is not God. Only as we live according to this Beatitude can we begin our ascent to the Kingdom of Heaven. The rich young ruler would never begin the ascent at all, (Mark 10:21) and the successful farmer who planned to build bigger barns to store his produce was called a fool by the Lord. (Luke 12:16-31)

The Jesus Prayer may show us the door to the Kingdom of Heaven which St. John Chrysostom tells us is the door to our own heart.(18) But know this! Neither the Jesus Prayer nor any other spiritual exercise will aid us along the way to "self-actualization," as the various human potential movements would have it. The Jesus Prayer will not help us to "find" ourselves, or improve ourselves. The way of the Jesus prayer is not to ourselves, but through ourselves, that we may find in our deepest selves the place where God is.(19) This is the summit of the interior mountain, and it is found in that secret place which we cannot find but through entire surrender of the self.

"Blessed are those who mourn, for they shall be comforted."
(Matt. 5:5)

Our ascent to the summit of Christian Perfection must begin with a sense of sin. This ought not surprise us, inasmuch as Christianity itself begins with a sense of sin. "Lord Jesus Christ, Son of God, have mercy on me a sinner," is the response of a person who is heartbroken for what his or her sin has done to God and Jesus Christ, to the world, to the community and to the self. The Fathers use the word "compunction" to speak of this sorrow. The word comes from "to puncture" which is the same action that nailed Jesus to the cross. Compunction is a puncturing of the heart.

Compunction is more than a twinge of misgiving. It is more than anxiety arising from an awareness of guilt. It is the sorrow that brings ache to the heart and unrestrained tears to the eyes. It is like one's mourning for the dead, and yet it brings what William Barclay calls "an amazing kind of bliss."(20) This bliss comes as we experience the cleansing of our heart, a cleansing that David praises in Psalm 51:17: "My sacrifice, O God, is this broken spirit; you will not despise this wounded heart."

The theme of sacrifice is further expressed by St. John Climacus who speaks of sorrow or mourning as "the typical pain of a soul on fire"(21), and counsels his monks about how to receive it:

"Hold fast to the blessed and joyful sorrow of holy compunction and do not cease laboring for it until it lifts you high above the things of the world to present you, a cleansed offering, to Christ."(22)

For the person who practices the Jesus Prayer, this "holy compunction," or "blessed and joyful sorrow" may well be inevitable. This is what the Fathers call "the gift of tears." This is why the discipline of the Jesus Prayer is best undertaken as part of a supportive fellowship, or under the supervision of a spiritual director. Christians committed to bear one another's burdens provide a redemptive environment wherein the gift of tears may do its cleansing work, whereas the solitary petitioner is likely to become mired in a slough of despond. When this occurs, the spiritual benefit derived from the gift of tears is diminished, or lost altogether.

Several Christmases ago, at the end of one of those calendar years where Christmas Eve falls on a Sunday, my congregation was consumed by the cycle of excessive preparation. We all, as the poet suggests, were in the midst of "grossly overestimating our powers."(23)

At ten minutes to nine on that Christmas Eve morning, the adult Sunday School teacher—conveniently, I thought at the time—came down with a bout of laryngitis. His class was to be full of visitors as well as some of the more wayward members, who were "making their Christmas."

Having made no preparation for the traditional forty-five minute lecture, I frantically looked about my study for something that would enable me to pull the proverbial rabbit from the hat. Alas, neither rabbit nor hat was to be found. But there was an icon of Our Lady of Tenderness, hanging on the wall. (Figure 1) In a flash I knew what I would do. I would ask the class to contemplate the icon for twenty minutes, lead a series of discussion questions on "what the icon means to me," close the session with a prayer, and then, hopefully, the bell would ring. I did not yet know it, but before the bell would ring, something extraordinary would take place.

Given the fact that the class was not accustomed to contemplating icons, I explained the exercise with an amazing lack of trepidation, and we sat, gazing at the icon for twenty minutes.

After the allotted time had elapsed, an elderly woman volunteered that she saw the Virgin Mary handing over the baby Jesus to be crucified by the class. After that somewhat startling statement, she burst into tears. A considerate but usually no-nonsense business-man attempted to divert the attention of the class with a less "loaded" statement, but found himself too overcome to continue. I looked at my hastily-prepared discussion questions through mist-covered eyes and discovered that I myself could not speak. For the entire class period, the assembly sat in silence, and by the end of it, everyone was quietly sobbing. When the bell rang, everyone filed-out without saying a word. No one ever mentioned the incident again, but the silence was not out of embarrassment. Some experiences are so cleansing that they are simply beyond words.

Geared as we Protestants are to words and their effects, we may be tempted to look at the proverbial "bottom-line" and ask, "As a result of that experience, how many accepted Christ as their personal Savior?" or, more to the point, "How many of the participants renewed their commitment to the church in a 'tangible' way?" I honestly do not know the answers to these questions. I only know that in a strange

Figure 1

and unexpected way, forty people received the gift of tears, and each went his or her way cleansed. The Christian life, like the Jesus Prayer, is a balance between hope and fear. Yet, we cannot be ruled by fear and shame, but by thankfulness and love.(24) As fear and shame are usually self-inflicted, we desperately need our balance restored by the community of faith, which mediates thankfulness and love.

With the gift of tears comes hope, for tears are a sign that the heart has been overwhelmed by the love of God.(25) Tears during prayer are "a sign of God's mercy...a sign that prayer is accepted and through tears has begun to enter the field of purity."(26) St. John Climacus makes the rather extraordinary statement that the tears that come after baptism often have a greater effect than the baptism itself:

"The baptism received by us as children we have all defiled, but we cleanse it anew with our tears. If God in His love for the human race had not given us tears, those being saved would be few, and hard to find."(27)

Yet, even so great a blessing as the gift of tears may be abused, and even marketed! I refer to the bogus, mascara-stained video tears which for a decade beguiled many well-meaning Christians, but cleansed no one. Apparently this is not just a phenomenon of the TV age, as the seventh-century saint tartly remarks:

"I have seen small teardrops shed like drops of blood, and I have seen floods of tears poured out with no trouble at all. So I judge toilers by their struggles, rather than their tears; and I suspect that God does so too."(28)

If one corruption of the gift of tears is perpetuated by the self-serving, another, more monstrous corruption is perpetuated by persons who are completely sincere. This corruption twists the work of the Holy Spirit in such a way as to drive the innocent to despair. Everyone who struggles along the way of the ascent to Christian Perfection must pass through a time of troubles, or a time of dryness, when God is perceived to be absent. Sometimes, the Fathers tell us, God even withdraws His blessings for awhile to bring us to our senses. Nicodemus of the Holy Mountain says: "As the eyes fail to see what is too near, but need a suitable distance, so ungrateful souls, when deprived of blessings, often become aware of former mercies."(29) The corruption comes when people take this belief too far, the claim being that the greater the sin, the greater the need for tears, and thus the need for something really terrible to happen!

58

In one of my parishes lived a young couple desperate to have a child. Three premature infants were born to them in the space of five years, and in spite of heroic measures each died after several weeks. As a consequence, the couple endured five years of alternating despair and hope. "I cannot understand what I must have done that God is punishing us so!" said the young husband in his grief. Throughout that period, more than a few well-meaning persons affirmed his notion of divine punishment, saying that it was all God's will.

There is an answer to this, and would that it would be heard on such occasions: "If it was not God's will that Jesus should die on the cross, how could it possibly be His will that these little ones should die?" Jesus revealed at the tomb of Lazarus that He Himself hated death, and this tells us that our Heavenly Father hates death as well. But we live in an imperfect world where death—unfortunately—has a part. Further, if the death of Christ accomplished a full, sufficient sacrifice for the sins of the whole world, we must conclude that it is morbid and unchristian to assert that the death of other persons is needed to atone for our sin! If we believe this, we underestimate the compassion of God and overestimate the gravity of our sins!

Many do, however, find that their spiritual energies are awakened in terrible circumstances, and that out of these circumstances they begin to live far more creative lives than many healthy—or lucky—persons who are spiritually asleep. Leslie Weatherhead puts the matter in perspective when he says that it is because the saints have reacted so positively to evil that the fallacy has got about that disease and death are the will of God.(30)

We must see the tears that the Jesus Prayer may bring, not as something we deserve, but as something, apart from the grace of God, we do not deserve, for tears are a resplendent gift from the Holy Spirit.(31) They are meant to puncture and transform our deepest selves.

The Second Beatitude contains the same balance as the Jesus Prayer itself. It tells us that although we are sinners in need of repentance, we need not get stuck in a slough of despond. The Beatitude, like the Jesus Prayer, is not the end of the road, but the beginning of the ascent to God. The person transformed by the gift of tears never ceases to make progress in the away of ascent, but the person who denies these tears never begins the journey at all!

59

"Blessed are the meek for they shall inherit the earth." (Matt. 5.5)

St. John Climacus says of the gift of tears that tears of genuine mourning will extinguish the very flame of anger.(32) This, he continues, leads to meekness, which is the blessing of the Third Beatitude: "Meekness is a permanent condition of that soul which remains unaffected by whether or not it is spoken well of, whether or not it is honored or praised."(33)

Unfortunately, in the English-speaking world, meekness is not a virtue to which many aspire, inasmuch as it seems to imply a deficiency of spirit and courage. Yet, while this word appears in the Greek Old Testament, it conveys anything but these deficiencies. We are told in Numbers 12:3 that "Moses was very meek, more than all men that were on the face of the earth." (RSV) Yet Moses was courageous, single-minded in devotion to his God and attentive to His promises. Psalm 37:11 indicates that it is the meek of Moses's ilk that will inherit the land of promise, whereas the wicked will be no more. Christian meekness is neither weakness nor lack of principle. Leech names it a strong virtue which requires a great inner strength.(34)

The word that Matthew uses which the Authorized Version translates as "meek" is the Greek word praus, the regular word for an animal that has been domesticated, and has been trained to respond to the yoke. This is the yoke Jesus invites all to shoulder who would call upon His name. (Matthew 11:29)

Those who strive to make the Jesus Prayer part of their devotional life pray in the spirit of the great Wesleyan hymn:

Give me to bear the easy yoke,
And every moment watch and pray;
and still to things eternal look,
and hasten to the glorious day.(35)

The Third Beatitude says in effect: "Blessed is the person who has surrendered every passion to God's control. There is no end to the blessing that such a person receives, be it in the promised land or the restored earth of the Messianic Age."

To strive to make the Jesus Prayer a part of our life is to move in the direction of entire surrender to Christ. The first word of the prayer, "Lord," had a particularly strong meaning at the beginning, when emperor worship monopolized its use in an idolatrous way.(36) In the time of Paul there were "Lords many." "Yet," he says, "for us there is one God, the Father, from whom are all things and for whom we exist, and one Lord Jesus Christ through whom are all things and through whom we exist." (I Corinthians 8:5 RSV)

Although the Jesus of the Jesus Prayer will brook no rivals, the mercies that He promises all who call upon Him are great to overflowing. These blessings were enumerated long ago by Origen, who said: "The name of Jesus frees people from mental distraction, puts devils to flight, cures the sick; it infuses a wonderful meekness and tranquility of character, love for mankind, and kindness and gentleness."(37)

When I was a young boy and ready for confirmation, my pastor often spoke about the assurance of the Spirit, of which these gifts are a part. This assurance, he believed, was required of all who would join the church. He informed us that after our period of preparation was completed he would meet with us individually at the altar and inquire as to the state of our souls.

The dread day, when it dawned, would have been alive with possibilities but for the dead hand of the church. The winter's snow had finally melted and my buddies were going to bike out to the railroad bridge to a "fort" we had built the previous summer. Unfortunately, my "examination" had eliminated that pleasant possibility. I entered the dark sanctuary and sat at the minister's feet. After about forty minutes of total silence he asked, "Do you feel Him calling?" What I heard was the ring of bicycle bells. Although by then it was late afternoon, my buddies were still circling the block, waiting for me! "I feel it, Reverend!" I fibbed. His sad eyes looked into mine as he said, "You'll have to write this time and date in your confirmation Bible, so that later you'll look back and remember. Do you understand?" "Yes, Reverend" I replied, leaving the gloom as quickly as I could without being rude. That day I would soar, not Godward in the Spirit, but riverward on my bike. I thought that I had put one over on the Reverend, but the date and time he had me inscribe in my Confirmation Bible is still there. April 21, 1956 at 4:50 PM may have been the beginning of an awakening after all, or at least the beginning of my attention. The Fathers knew that the ordinary state of the human soul is "an unwakable sleep identical with death."(38) The soul may begin to awaken, however, as the mind rouses it by means of the name of Jesus.

It is the attentive life in which the Jesus Prayer may begin and to which it strives. This attentive life, according to Hesychius of Jerusalem:"...is the father of contemplation and knowledge and the origin of Divine ascents and wise thoughts. As the prophet Isaiah says, 'they that wait upon the Lord shall renew their strength; they shall mount up with wings as eagles.' " (Isaiah 40:31) (39)

The attentive life, which is the door to Christian spirituality, was embodied by this same Old Testament prophet. The story of his approach to the altar, writes Evelyn Underhill

"...is a story so well known that we easily take it for granted, and so fail to realize it as one of the most magnificent and significant in the world, for it shows us the awakening of a human being to his true situation over against reality, and the true object of his fugitive life. There are three stages to it. First, the sudden disclosure of the Divine Splendour; the mysterious and daunting beauty of Holiness, on which even the seraphs dare not look. The veil is lifted, and the reality which is always there is revealed. And at once the young man sees, by contrast, his own dreadful imperfection. 'Woe is me! for I am a man of unclean lips!' The vision of perfection, if it is genuine, always brings shame, penitence, and therefore purification. That is the second stage. What is the third? The faulty human creature, who yet possesses the amazing power of saying Yes or No to the Eternal God, is asked for his services, and instantly responds. 'Who will go for us?' 'Here am I! Send me!' "(40)

In this encounter with the holy, the threefold essence of the spiritual life comes into focus. First, there is the vision of the Perfect, which is contained in "Lord Jesus Christ, Son of God..." Then there is the sense of imperfection and unworthiness against the Perfect which always follows, expressed by "have mercy on me, a sinner." And then, "Because of the vision, and in spite of the imperfection, action in the interest of the Perfect—cooperation with God."(41)

Evelyn Underhill tells us that in addition to being receivers of the vision, we become its transmitters. This is accomplished in a three-fold manner: by our continuing contemplation, by our action in the world, and our continuous self-opening to God. We must keep ourselves sensitive to His music and light but also the needs of our fellow-creatures. This tension, she continues, ought to form "one life; mediating between God and His world, and bringing the saving power of the Eternal into time."(42)

Meekness is entire self-giving, sacrifice, struggle and effort on behalf of the vision, and spiritual transformation over time. Far from being a deficiency of spirit or courage, this meekness is one of the strong virtues. It is an inner strength which equips the spirit to undertake the journey of ascent no matter what the cost.

The Jesus Prayer may awaken in us that vision of Perfection encountered by Isaiah. It is a vision upon which: "...the awakened soul gazes as a magnet, drawing him toward itself. It means effort, faithfulness, courage, and sometimes grim encounters if he is to respond to that attraction, and move towards it along the narrow track which leads up and out from the dark valleys of the mind..."(43)

"Blessed are those who hunger and thirst for righteousness, for they shall be satisfied." (Matt. 5:6)

Consciousness of sin, Paul Tillich observes, is experienced as a state of separation, alienation and estrangement: "We know that we are estranged from something to which we really belong, and to which we should be united."(44)

Existence itself is separation. This is something we may have always known, or at least felt, for separation begins in the mother's womb! We are separated from ourselves, from our fellow creatures, and from God. The creature longs to be reunited with the Creator, but finds itself lost. It is like the sensation described by W.H. Auden in "For the Time Being":

alone, alone about a dreadful wood
of conscious evil runs a lost mankind...(45)

In the Fourth Beatitude, Our Lord likens this state of separation to one of hunger and thirst. We who may never have seen a desert or wanted for food and water may fail to appreciate the sense of desperation the images of hunger and thirst suggested to the disciples. Desperation, however, we do know as a spiritual reality!

Tillich describes this reality as walking through the dark valley of a meaningless and empty life. It is having to bear the intolerable strain of disgust for our own being. It is having to endure our own indifference, weakness and hostility, lack of direction and composure. It is waiting year after year for the longed-for Perfection to appear, and enduring the old compulsions which continue to reign within. It is watching with passivity as despair continues to destroy joy and courage.(46)

Although Jesus frames this Beatitude—as all the others—in terms of promise and fulfillment, He may in truth be asking us a question, and a hard one at that: "How much do you desire the blessing of union with your Creator? Do you want it as desperately as the person dying of thirst wants water, or the person starving to death wants food? How intense is your desire for the reunion of life with life, and self with the deepest self? Do you cry out to God day and night? Do you beat your breast like a publican and plead, God be merciful to me, a sinner?" In truth, it is only the person who is hollow and knows it who can be filled!

The way of ascent is not an unconscious process, but presupposes an unceasing vigilance of spirit and a constant effort of the will.(47) "Lord Jesus Christ, Son of God, have mercy on me a sinner!" begins as an effort of the will and contributes to this unceasing vigilance of the spirit. The attention the Jesus Prayer makes possible contributes to our understanding that we must continually repent of our sins with the full realization that we may expect temptations until we draw our last breath.(48) It is a vigilance described by Hesychius of Jerusalem as: "...when the mind stands upright and calls upon Christ against its enemies, and runs to Him for refuge, it is like some wild animal, surrounded by many hounds, courageously facing them from the cover of its shelter. It discerns mentally from afar the mental ambushes of its unseen enemies, for it continually prays to the peace-giving Jesus for His help."(49)

Constant effort of the will is required. St. Macarius of Egypt sees this as the essential condition, inasmuch as without it, God does nothing.(50) Wesley is of the same mind, as he states in one of his sermons, "The Righteousness of Faith": "...the only means under heaven given to a man whereby he may regain...the image of God, which is the true life of the soul, is submitting to the righteousness which is of faith, the believing in the only begotten Son of God."(51)

Given that the natural state of our spirit borders on sleep, it would seem that this "believing on the only begotten Son of God" would include constant prayer and attention. This is certainly the thrust of the famous Wesleyan hymn:

I want a principle within
of watchful, godly fear,
a sensibility of sin,
a pain to feel it near.

64

Help me the first approach to feel
of pride or wrong desire,
To catch the wandering of my will,
and quench the kindling fire.(52)
Charity, the greatest of the virtues, is the fruit of constant prayer and its essential completion. It is through the action of prayer and charity that the mystical union is accomplished.(53)

The Fourth Beatitude seems, for those who cannot tolerate a mystery, to raise the question of the relationship between faith and works. The paradox it expresses—"Does hungering and thirsting after righteousness gain the blessing of being filled?"—is put into focus by a great Russian bishop who says, "The Holy Ghost, acting within us, accomplishes with us our salvation," but, "..being assisted by grace, man accomplishes the work of his salvation."(54)

The Protestant problem with this question stems from John's image of the vine and the branches where Jesus says, "apart from me you can do nothing."(15:5) The source of salvation is never human-kind itself, but God. St. John acknowledges this in his First Epistle where he says that love comes from God. (I:4:7) Yet this gift is for nothing unless there resides a corresponding disposition in created nature, "a germ or potentiality for love in the human being called to attain his own perfection in love."(55) Wesley, recognizing this poten-tiality, says: "There is no man that is in a state of mere nature; there is no man...that is wholly void of the grace of God. No man living is utterly destitute of...natural conscience."(56)

It is this "natural conscience" that hungers and thirsts after right-eousness, that yearns for reunion and completion. This is what St. Augustine means when he says: "You awake us to delight in your praise; for You made us for Yourself, and our hearts are restless until they rest in You."(57)

The Fourth Beatitude implies a combined action or cooperation between the creature and the Creator. Human-kind hungers and thirsts for righteousness, and is filled, through the action of the Spirit. The person who begins the journey of ascent receives from the Spirit both the desire and the power to act. "Direct knowledge of God," affirms Nicodemus of the Holy Mountain, "is a gift of God, conscience is a gift of God, thirst for heavenly life is a gift of God. These three constitute the spirit of our life, urging us heavenward."(58) But, lest we take pride in our own achievements, he says in another place,

"Strive with all diligence but expect success only from God's help."(59)

Grace is a divine gift, yet strangely, the more we acquire it, the greater effort it demands of us. Once we begin to be sensitized by grace, the more we hunger for justice for all creatures, not just ourselves. The more grace we receive, the more we yearn for completion, not just for ourselves, but for all creatures. Many for whom the Jesus Prayer has taken hold in their lives find themselves more compassionate. The more compassionate we become, the greater the likelihood that we would be consumed by the demands we come increasingly to place upon ourselves, but for fresh supplies of grace.

Persons who practice the Jesus Prayer find that not all hungers end in self-disgust. Our hunger for Perfection, coming as it does from the Father of Lights, lead inexorably to higher hungers accompanied by new sensitivities. This is a process that continues until the Resurrection. As Isaac the Syrian says, "there are no bounds to perfection, for even the perfection of the most perfect is naught but imperfection. Hence, until the moment of death neither times nor works of repentance can ever be complete."(60)

Evelyn Underhill tells us that this hunger—this longing for God—is the seed from which grows the fruitful plant of prayer. The Jesus Prayer may be the response of our deepest self to the attraction of the Perfect. It may be a means to awaken in us "the recognition that He made us for Himself, that we depend on Him and are meant to depend on Him, and that we shall not know the meaning of peace until our communion with Him is at the center of our lives."(61)

Twenty years ago, many of our congregations adopted liturgical banners, almost without reservation. I remember designing one of these for use in worship. It bore the famous Robert Louis Stevenson quotation: "To travel hopefully is a better thing than to arrive." I now realize that, at the time, the statement expressed what amounted to the sum-total of my religious experience. I have come to realize that belief in nothing more than what amounts to a slick cliché in the midst of our hunger and thirst for righteousness, is a kind of Gethsemane.

The Fourth Beatitude, brought into focus by the Jesus Prayer, shows us a deeper reality: we may travel hopefully and actually catch glimpses of the summit at the same time. More than this, as our unveiled faces begin to reflect the brightness of the Lord, we will grow brighter and brighter as we gradually turn into the image that we reflect. (I Cor. 3:18) With our eyes ever gazing upon the summit, we may say with the Psalmist:

"For the reward of virtue is to see your face, and on awakening, to gaze my fill on your likeness." (Psalm 17:15)

"Blessed are the merciful, for they shall obtain mercy." (Matt. 5:7)

The Fifth Beatitude tells us that the merciful shall have mercy shown to them. As none of the Beatitudes place limits on the blessings promised, I take it to mean that these blessings will be on-going. The blessing of mercy, like the ascent itself, never ends!

In Matthew's Gospel, Jesus tells a story about a servant who owed his master an astronomical sum of money—millions of dollars in today's currency. As the servant had no means of paying, the master gave orders that he, his wife and children, be sold into slavery to meet the debt. But because the servant threw himself at his master's feet, and begged so piteously to be given more time, the master was moved to pity, cancelled the debt, and let him go.

Going out, Jesus continues, the man fell upon a fellow-servant who owed him twenty dollars or less, but no amount of pleading would prevent this ungrateful servant from having his debtor thrown into prison. Hearing of this, the master had the ungrateful servant bound and handed him over to the torturers until he should pay every penny. (Matt. 18:23-35)

This tells us that if we throw ourselves at the feet of our Lord, beseeching Him to "have mercy on me, a sinner!" we may expect that mercy will be given. This mercy, however, has a price, and if we prove unwilling to pay that price, we shall find that the mercy we expected to receive as a matter of course will be denied us. As Nicodemus of the holy Mountain reminds us: "You should come to prayer bringing deeds corresponding to your petition, and after prayer work still harder to become worthy to receive the grace and virtue that you ask for."(62)

Although we have been speaking about Christian Perfection as the way of ascent, it has a horizontal as well as a vertical plane. Evelyn Underhill tells us that our gaze must extend both vertically to God and horizontally to other souls, and "the more it grows in both directions, the less merely individual and therefore the more truly personal it will be."(63) If we would reach what she calls the everlasting snows, we must never avert our gaze from our neighbor in need. If we are not always prepared to share the mercy we ourselves have received from

God, we will surely lose our way. We must continually remember James's words to the church that there will be judgment without mercy to those who themselves have not been merciful. (2:13)

The mercy of the Jesus Prayer is so rich a blessing that the Greek language must employ two words to express it. The phrase, "have mercy," uttered by the two blind men in the Gospel of Matthew, is expressed by the word eleison, which denotes compassionate mercy or pity. The publican in Luke, however, uses a different word in his prayer: *ilaothete,* which is a plea for healing reconciliation or pardon. Although both *pity* and *pardon* are gathered up in the English word *mercy,* they are not precisely the same. Pity is what we may feel for the suffering innocent. Pardon is what we may extend to someone who has harmed us but who in our judgment may be deserving of another chance. At any rate, when the publican asks for pardon rather than pity, Luke is introducing the action of the mystery of our redemption.(64) Pity and pardon are set in contrast, albeit unwittingly, by the penitent thief who says: "We got the same sentence as He did, but we deserved it: we're paying for what we did, but this man has done nothing wrong." (Luke 23:40-41)

When we are first led to prayer "Lord Jesus Christ, Son of God, have mercy on me, a sinner," we may be asking for pity. Perhaps we are convinced that we have been despitefully used, abused, and treated unfairly by the world. The publican, as we have noted, does not ask for pity. Why? Because he has committed all his extortions with his eyes open, and he is aware that it is pardon that he needs. This is the beginning of true repentance, clarity and spiritual maturity. True repentance, says St. John Climacus, "is the admission that all our troubles, and more besides, whether visible or not, were richly deserved."(65)

Until we possess the clarity of the publican, we have the spiritual development of a child. Bishop Ignatius reminds us:

"A child in spiritual growth is unfit for spiritual gifts. He will use them not for the glory of God, not for the benefit of himself and his neighbors, not for defeating unseen foes; but he will use them to strike himself, will become conceited and filled with fatal pride and ruinous scorn for his neighbors."(66)

John Wesley tells us in the Covenant Service that we must repent of our thoughtless judgments, hasty condemnations and grudging forgiveness if ever we are to become instruments of God's mercy.(67)

When we discover that these preoccupations no longer consume the amount of energy and time that they once did, it may be because the Jesus Prayer has begun to do its work. Then we will discover that we are free from those inordinate desires, fears and anxieties which are at the root of our anger and unhappiness.

In general, Helmut Thielicke observes, "we human beings live according to the echo principle—what you do to me, I do to you."(68) But for those who toil in the way of ascent, mercy dwells in the heart prior to the deed. Mercy, like sin, is a state before it is an act:

The quality of mercy is not strain'd,
It droppeth as the gentle rain from heaven
Upon the place beneath: it is twice blest;
It blesseth him that gives and him that takes:
'Tis mightiest in the mightiest: it becomes
The throned monarch better than his crown.
(The Merchant of Venice, Act IV, Scene 1)

The merciful are so because they are too aware of their own sins to be shocked by the sins of others. They never stop examining themselves, never cease mourning for their own sins, and never cease crying out to the Lord for mercy. Thus it is that they draw down upon themselves the tender mercies of God. They receive as they give, and when bitterness would cloud their vision of the summit, they surrender that bitterness to the Lord. "Blessed are the pure in heart, for they shall see God."(Matt. 5:8)

When Yuri Gagarin, the first Soviet cosmonaut, returned from space, he is said to have remarked that he didn't see God in heaven. Soon afterward, a Moscow priest of the Orthodox church is said to have demurred, "If you have not seen Him on earth, you will never see Him in heaven."(69) It is a simple fact that we see only what we are prepared to see. This is true of physical objects, and it is also true of spiritual realities.

The Sixth Beatitude proclaims without qualification that the pure in heart shall see God. It makes no distinction between the future near at hand and that Great Future which awaits beyond the borders of the Resurrection. Thus, it seems to contradict the Old Testament belief that no one can look upon the face of God and live. (Ex. 33:20) Yet, even if this belief seems to be somewhat "modified" by the Sixth Beatitude, the New Testament remains as uncompromising as the Old:

"No one has ever seen God; it is the only Son, who is nearest to the Father's heart, who has made him known." (John 1:18)

If we are promised that we will meet God "face to face" while here below, it is through prayer that this meeting will take place. One of the ways this takes place is through the Prayer of Jesus: "I am the Way, the Truth and the Life. No one can come to the Father except through me." (John 14:6)

To pray the Jesus Prayer, "Lord Jesus Christ, Son of God, have mercy on me, a sinner," is to enter into a personal relationship with God and to come before His presence.

But what is the pure heart, and how does it prepare us to see God? Although the ancients believed that the heart was the seat of the emotions, intellect and will, everyone now knows that the heart muscle is nothing more than an efficient albeit necessary pump. But the ancients were not talking "physiology." When they spoke of the heart they were using the language of metaphor to express the mystery of the deepest self.

The belief-system that gave rise to the Jesus Prayer held that the discipline of prayer made the heart ready to receive the infusion of grace. To pray the prayer constantly was to "guard the heart." This effort took seriously the claim that only the pure in heart would see God. Although the "physiology" seems outmoded, the belief-system is surely not! What do we mean when we exclaim, "I thought my heart would break!" We are saying, "It was as though everything that makes me what I am: emotions, intellect and will — everything — was being ripped apart!" The naive physiology notwithstanding, agitation and turmoil were as real to the ancients as they are to us. It is to this that Jesus refers when he says, "Do not let your hearts be troubled or afraid." (John 14:27)

To guard the heart is to keep agitation and turmoil away from the center of our being so that the Spirit of God might dwell therein. This is the work of the Jesus Prayer. To guard the heart St. Simeon says, "You should observe three things above all else: freedom from all cares; not only cares about bad and vain but even about good things, or in other words, you should become dead to everything; your conscience should be clear in all things, so that it denounces you in nothing; you should have complete absence of passionate attachments so that your thought inclines to nothing worldly."(70)

70

This state of silence is both the starting-point and the final achievement of the practice of the Prayer of Jesus. It is a state that Metropolitan Anthony describes as the complete peace of all the faculties of the body and the powers of the soul. In this state, everything is quiet and recollected, perfectly alert and free from agitation.(71)

He goes on to describe this state as being like the waters of a pond. If the mud at the bottom is in motion, there can be no clear vision through it. If the surface of the pond is covered with ripples, there can be no accurate reflection of what surrounds it.(72) Inasmuch as God is the source of everything and in everything, it is only the pure in heart—those persons who are free from inner agitation and turmoil—who will see God.

When stillness has brought us to the place where we may experience the presence of God, another sort of stillness intervenes. This is a condition of silence or tranquility that the Fathers describe as "astonishment," or "wonder," or "ravishing."(73) Sometimes this is called "ecstasy," and in it a person seems to leave his or her own life, for the life to come.(74) It is this state to which Paul refers in 2 Corinthians 12:2-4. It is a state wherein the spiritual traveler becomes conscious that he or she belongs to God and surrenders to His Spirit.

The Fathers caution the spiritual traveler to be wary of ecstasies and ravishments, inasmuch as every spirit is not the Holy Spirit. These things, as the experience of Paul testifies, may be more a part of the beginning of the ascent than the ongoing experience of those who make progress in the way.

St. Simeon compares this ecstasy to the condition of a person born in a dark prison which is feebly lit by a single lamp. This person has no conception, either of the light of the sun or the beauty of the world outside. If the sunlight suddenly penetrates through a crack in the wall of such a prison, this person will experience ecstasy. In time, however, the senses become accustomed to the sunlight, and if the prisoner would be released from prison, the eyes would soon adjust to a world that otherwise would be too terrifying to contemplate. In the same way, the soul "which progresses in the spiritual life no longer knows ecstasies: instead it has the constant experience of the divine reality in which it lives."(75)

Lev Gillet refers to this as a "habitual state of luminosity," which is the fruit of constant or frequent practice of the Jesus Prayer.(76) This, he continues, "is more than a symbol; it is less than a sensible perception, and it is certainly not an ecstasy; but it is something real, although indescribable."(77)

The promise of the Sixth Beatitude is that through prayer we shall "see" God. This means that we will be conscious of the presence of God at every stage of the ascent. When all the faculties of the body are at peace, and when we are free from inner agitation and turmoil, we will stand like Elijah on the mountain of God. After the earthquake, wind and fire have done their work, we will encounter the still, small voice of the Father. (I Kings 19:22)

St. Simeon, in his hymn to love, is clear that this presence is revealed, not for its own sake, but to equip the spiritual traveler for the work of God: "O holy love, he who knows thee not has never tasted the sweetness of thy mercies which only living experience can give us. But he who has known thee, or has been known by thee, can never again have even the smallest doubt. For thou art the fulfillment of the Law, thou who fillest, burnest, enkindlest, embracest my heart with measureless charity. Thou art the teacher of the prophets, the offspring of the Apostles, the strength of the martyrs, the inspiration of Fathers and Doctors, the perfecting of all the Saints. And thou, O Love, preparest even me for the true service of God."(78)

"Blessed are the peacemakers, for they shall be called sons of God." (Matt. 5:9)

Every person who is in a state of separation or alienation from God is, to some extent, "a walking civil war."(79) Many find, however, that as the Jesus Prayer begins to penetrate the totality of their lives, this inner warfare beings to abate. Then they reach the stage of the climb where "ills have no weight, and tears no bitterness."(80)

Persons who receive the gift of peace find within themselves the capacity to bring the good tidings of great joy to a fragmented world. Persons who have received the gift of peace are peacemakers by their very presence. Such a person may be ordained or unordained, a monk, nun or layworker in the church. He or she may be wise or simple. Yet he or she, as Alexander Solzhenitsyn suggests in his story *Matryona's House*, is ...that one righteous person without whom, as the saying goes, no city can stand.(81)

In the continuing life of the Christian community it soon becomes evident to the people of God that there are persons within that community who have been given the gift of peace. In every congregation I have ever served, there have been a score of such persons. Once, however, I served a congregation where there was only one such person, and when she died, chaos ensued!

Obviously, the gift of peace and peacemaking is not bestowed by God willy-nilly, but must be the fruit of a life of discipline and prayer. Thus it is never an accident that this or that person shows up as a peacemaker. Such a life may begin with the Jesus Prayer.

The Fathers held that this prayer, when connected with one's breathing, sobriety, and unfailing memory of death and humility,(82) brings into proper balance the body, mind and spirit. Without this inner harmony there can be no peace, and thus no capacity for peacemaking.

Inner peace, which is the fruit of contemplation, must express itself by way of deeds, or action. The way of peace, like the way of ascent itself, must include both this inner and outer dynamic, or the spiritual traveler will lose his or her way and fall headlong. This necessary balance between the "inner" and the "outer" is expressed by St. John:

> Whoever says, 'I love God,'
> and hates his brother
> is a liar.
> How can a man who does not love the brother he sees
> love God, whom he has not seen?
> This is the commandment He has given us:
> 'Anyone who loves God must also love his brother.'
> (I John 4:20-21)

Wesley cautions us in the same spirit saying, "Holy solitaries are like holy adulterers."

The gift of peace comes through the action of the Holy Spirit, yet it must be "attained." We must work for it, and through a surrender that looks like this: "Perish every fond ambition, all I've sought or hoped or known..."(83)

For there to be a cessation of hostilities there must be a surrender. We must surrender to God if the civil war that rages within is to come to an end, and we are to receive the gift of peace.

The beginning of surrender is to learn to be alone with God, and we know that aloneness is a state that many of us will do almost anything to avoid. We may remember the catchy song from *The King and I* that goes:

> Whenever I feel afraid,
> I hold my head erect

and whistle a happy tune
so no one will suspect I'm afraid.(84)

The Jesus Prayer, unlike the "happy tune" proferred by the world, makes us aware of a real presence which calls us, enfolds us, strengthens us, and beckons us ever upward. Being alone with God does not require a retreat from the world, for the practice of the Prayer teaches us that we can stand alone before God even in the midst of a life of service to the world. In the mist of the world, the Jesus Prayer enables us to listen to the stillness of our deepest selves and the "wordless speech of the Spirit."(85) It is here that we learn the truth, that we are utterly and groundlessly loved.

With this truth comes peace, and this peace leads us to a heightened awareness. Part of this awareness, observes Kallistos Ware, is the recognition that we are unable to heal the wounds of the world solely through social programs, psychiatry or common sense. "Our complacency is broken down, we appreciate our own inadequacy, and start to understand what Christ meant by the 'one thing necessary.' " (86)

The gift of peace making comes of the prior gift of inner peace. Yet even this inner peace comes of a still earlier gift, and that is the gift of discernment. Discernment is "the ability to perceive intuitively the secret of another's heart, to understand the hidden depths of which the other is unaware."(87) St. John Climacus calls this "a solid understanding of the will of God in all times, in all places, in all things—and it is found only among those who are pure in heart, in body, and in speech."(88) This capacity is neither ESP nor clairvoyance, but the fruit of "concentrated prayer and unremitting struggle."(89)

The gift of discernment gives wings to the gift of peace inasmuch as it makes possible two actions in the world. The peacemaker is given the capacity to love others and to make their sufferings his or her own. In addition, the peacemaker is given the capacity to transform both the human and natural environments.(90)

First, the peacemaker loves others and makes their sufferings his or her own. This is the living-out of compassion which literally means, "to suffer with." Compassion flies in the face of that conventional wisdom which says that the effective counselor is a detached counselor. Detachment does protect the counselor from becoming personally involved and thus contributes to a kind of objectivity. The peacemaker, on the other hand, cannot avoid becoming personally involved because he or she knows intuitively that persons who do not love others have little power to heal them.(91) And the peacemaker is objective! He or she knows what love costs! Yet, he or she also knows that the love which is of God carries with it its own empowerment.

"It is an abyss of illumination, a fountain of fire, bubbling up to inflame the thirsty soul. It is the condition of angels and the progress of eternity."(92)

The Jesus Prayer engages us in the action of compassion. Through this action we receive the fresh supplies of grace that such an expenditure requires.

Peacemaking also includes the power to transform the human and natural environments. When I first began to "write" icons, I noticed that the vestibule of my instructor's house was always filled with plastic garbage bags. Later, when I happened to catch a glimpse of him picking-up empty aluminum cans along the riverfront, I realized what the bags contained. I suspect that this gentle soul went about this enterprise, not primarily to make money in the recycling business, but to express his love for Creation. Those who have the power to trans- form both the human and natural environments have received the power to discern the universal presence of the Creator, and to assist others to perceive it.(93) St. Isaac the Syrian describes this gift in his hymn to the merciful heart:

"What is the merciful heart? It is a heart that burns with love for the whole creation—for men, for the birds, for the beasts, for the demons, for every creature. When a man with such a heart as this thinks of the creatures, or looks at them, his eyes are filled with tears. An overwhelming compassion makes his heart grow small and weak, and he cannot endure to hear or see any suffering, even the smallest pain, inflicted upon any creature. Therefore, he never ceases to pray, with tears even for the irrational animals, for the enemies of truth, and for those who do him evil, asking that they may be guarded and receive God's mercy. And for the reptiles also he prays with a great compas- sion which rises up endlessly in his heart until he shines again and is glorious like God."(94)

The peacemaker must be continually at prayer that the gift of discernment he or she has received be creative of peace and not destructive to it. Knowledge is power, and a knowledge which is not bridled by compassion will certainly give free rein to the demonic.

The staretz Zosima, in Dostoevsky's *The Brothers Karamazov* sees the danger of the gift of discernment run amok. "At some ideas," he says, "you stand perplexed, especially at the sight of men's sin, uncertain whether to combat it by force or by humble love. Always decide, 'I will combat it by humble love.' If you make up your mind about that once and for all, you can conquer the whole world. Loving humility is a terrible force; it is the strongest of all things and there is nothing like it."(95)

"Blessed are those who are persecuted for righteousness' sake, for theirs is the kingdom of heaven. Blessed are you when men revile you and persecute you and utter all kinds of evil against you falsely on my account. Rejoice and be glad, for your reward is great in heaven, for so men persecuted the prophets who were before you." (Matt. 5:10-12)

A life given to the practice of the Jesus Prayer is one way to answer the call to Christian Perfection and the way of ascent. Thereby one may discover the truth that makes one free from endless preoccupation with fears and anxieties. Through it one may discover freedom from the power of inordinate desires. Here is freedom from old compulsions which, even if they do not entirely disappear, at least they no longer reign. Moreover, we discover freedom from the corrosive effects of anger. The anger which remains is redirected, purified and cleansed. "Now," William Johnston observes, "it is the anger of one who has seen, and still sees, real injustice in his own life and that of others and refuses to countenance such evil. It is an anger which more properly could be called love of justice and is accompanied by a willingness to die in the cause of justice. In itself this is nothing more than a mystical experience. It is the living flame of love orientated toward action."(96)

As the Old Testament prophets shrank from tumultuous action but could not resist the living flame of love, a life given to the practice of the Jesus Prayer leads inevitably to engagement in the world. This inner Light, once it is fanned to a flame, transforms the practitioner into a "prophetical person." Prophetical people, Johnson says, "are often quite unpredictable, often they are socially unacceptable, strident, exaggerated, apparently unorthodox. Like Jeremiah they are often ridiculed and put in the stocks. Usually they are put to death, either literally or metaphorically. But the distinctive thing is the quality of their love which 'bears all things, believes all things, hopes all things, endures all things.' "(97)

Jesus warns the disciples in the Eighth Beatitude what they might expect, and in John's Gospel, tells them that hostility from the world makes them one with Him: "If the world hates you, remember that it hated me first" (John 15:18). St. John affirms this, telling Christians that they must not be surprised when they find that the world hates them. (I John 3:13-14) Paul, in his Second Epistle to Timothy, makes it even more emphatic when he says that everyone who desires to live a Godly life in Christ will be persecuted. (2 Timothy 3:12)

Simon Metaphrastes typifies the teaching of the later Fathers when he says that sufferings for righteousness' sake are not only to be expected and endured, but actually embraced:

"A soul bound by bonds of love to God regards sufferings as nothing, takes joy in sorrows and blossoms in grief. When it suffers nothing for the sake of its beloved, it thirsts still more for sufferings and flees from consolation as from torment."(98)

The one thing that is curious about the beginning of each of the Synoptic Gospels is that we the readers share with the demons the knowledge of who Jesus is. If the demons recognize the Son of God before those who are on the way to Truth, it is also true that those who are on the way to Truth recognize the demons before those who are on the way to destruction. Or, put another way, "the unconverted simply lack the depth and the vision to see the roots of the problems."(99) The person who has spent long hours in meditation and prayer has met the devil face to face. He or she has seen his or her own vulnerability and awful potential for evil. He or she has also become sensitized to suffering in the world because of the suffering experienced within the self.(100)

Some might conclude that what is being described here is hot-headedness. My father always used to counsel me not to "go off half-cocked." By this I think he meant, "Make your anger count," or at least, "Count the cost before you run off on some cause." Jesus certainly advised His disciples to count the cost. There comes a time, however, when calculation must cease. For if spirituality is real for the practitioner of the Jesus Prayer, he or she will gladly pay whatever cost the situation may demand. This is not the prodding of the ego, for that has been left behind. It is the prodding of the inner Light to which every spiritual traveler must—sooner or later—surrender.

Dietrich Bonhoeffer surrendered to this inner Light when he left the safety of New York's Union Seminary to witness for the confessing church in his native land. For Bonhoeffer, Hitler was the Antichrist, and National Socialism, a devilish form of national egotism and greed. He believed that human freedom is a grace granted for the conservation of moral values and the divine ordering of human life. Concerning the Eighth Beatitude, he wrote:

"This does not refer to the righteousness of God, but to suffering in a just cause, suffering for their own just judgments and actions. For it is by these that they who renounce possessions, fortune, rights, righteousness, honour and force for the sake of following Christ, will be distinguished from the world. The world will be offended at them, and so the disciples will be persecuted for righteousness' sake. Not recognition, but rejection is the reward they get from the world for their message and works."(101)

He was executed by a special order of Himmler at the Flossenburg Concentration Camp on April 9, 1945, a few days before it was liberated by the Allies.(102) John Chrysostom said that the church was born out of the wounded side of Christ. So too it must continually be reborn out of the wounded sides of its martyrs.

Circumstances may never force us to the place where surrender to the inner Light would place us in harm's way, but clear moral and political issues face us every day. The inner Light, fanned to a flame by the Jesus Prayer, will surely prod us to actions in accord with the truths and demands of the Christian faith! These choices, causes and actions, Evelyn Underhill suggests, will be those least tainted by self-interest, and will make for the increase of happiness, health, beauty and peace. They will cleanse and harmonize life, and they "must always be in accordance with the will of the Spirit which is drawing life to perfection."(103)

During the maelstrom of hatred and violence unleashed by the assassination of Dr. Martin Luther King, Jr., the witness of one person remains fixed in my mind. Maxine Rotz was the assistant Postmaster at Three Springs, Pennsylvania, where I was a student minister. The events of that terrible week left the residents angry and confused. It fell to Maxine to lower the flag to half-staff, the morning after President Johnson's decree. As she was doing so, a small, angry crowd gathered on the sidewalk. One woman, purple with rage, shouted, "It's pretty (expletive) bad when our flag—the flag for which our boys died—has to be lowered for that (expletive) n——! Maxine, still lowering the flag, responded in her quiet way, "The order came from the Postmaster General, but you can blame me if you want. I've got broad shoulders!"

"Well!" the woman shouted, "Look at the n—— lover! Why don't you go to Russia where you belong?"

Maxine's eyes fixed on those of the woman. There was compassion in them—the compassion one might have for a hurt and angry child. "Jesus was color blind," she said, "and because I love Him so, I guess I'd better be color blind too!"

The crowd dispersed, shamefaced. It had encountered the one righteous person without whom no city can stand.

Christ needs our witness, but unless that witness is fueled by the inner Light, it will be inauthentic and shrill. Unless the inner light shines in the deepest self, we cannot expect to be able to pay the price that witness may demand of us. Perhaps we will never be called upon to die for Christ, but we have certainly been called to live for Him, and that, over time, may prove far more difficult! It is only after we have done battle with the evil within that we find the power to stand firm, and this, not because there is a point to be made or something to prove, but because our Lord has told us that the person who stands firm to the end will be saved.

(1) Gillet, Lev, *The Jesus Prayer,* St. Vladimir's Seminary Press, Crestwood, NY, 10707, 1987, pps. 40-41.

(2) Nicodemus of the Holy Mountain (Ed), *Unseen Warfare,* the Spiritual Combat and Path to Paradise of Scupoli, Lorenzo, St. Vladimir's Seminary Press, Crestwood, NY, 10707, 1987, p. 239.

(3) *Ibid.,* p. 177.

(4) *Ibid.,* p. 17.

(5) *Ibid.,* p. 81.

(6) *Op. Cit,* Gillet, pps. 69-70.

(7) Garvey, John (Ed.), *Modern Spirituality: An Anthology,* Templegate Publishers, Springfield, IL, 1985, p. 81.

(8) Brianchaninov, Ignatius, *On the Prayer of Jesus,* (Fr. Lazarus, Trans.), John M. Watkins, London, 1965, p. 68.

(9) Kadloubovsky E., and Palmer G.E.H., *Writings From the Philokalia On Prayer of the Heart,* Faber and Faber, London-Boston, 1983, p. 222.

(10) *Ibid.,* p. 210.

(11) Underhill, Evelyn, *The Spiritual Life,* Mowbrays Popular Christian Paperback Series by A.R. Mowbray & Co., Ltd., St. Thomas House, Becket St., Oxford, OX1 1SJ, pps. 67-68.

(12) *Op. Cit,* Brianchaninov, p. 77, *St. Isaac the Syrian,* Ch. 78.

(13) Bloom, Anthony, *Beginning to Pray,* Paulist Press, 545 Island Road, Ramsey, NJ 07446, 1982, p. 178.

(14) *Ibid.,* p. 41.

(15) Leech, Kenneth, *True Prayer: An Invitation To Christian Spirituality,* Harper and Row, Publishers, San Francisco, 1980, p. 170

(16) Luibheid, Colm and Russell, Norman (Trans.), *John Climacus: The Ladder of Divine Ascent,* Paulist Press., 545 Island Rd., Ramsey, NJ 07446, 1982, p. 178.

(17) *Op. Cit.,* Bloom, p. 42.

(18) *Ibid.,* p. 46.

(19) *Ibid.,* p. 46.

(20) Barclay, William, *The Gospel of Matthew: Vol 1,* Westminster Press, Philadelphia, 1975, p. 93.

(21) *Op. Cit.,* Luibheid, p. 137.

(22) *Ibid.,* p. 137.

(23) Mendelson, Edward, *W.H. Auden: Collected Poems,* Vintage International, Vintage books, A Division of Random House Inc., New York, 1991, p. 399.

(24) *Op. Cit., Nicodemus to the Holy Mountain,* p. 20.

(25) Lossky, Vladimir, *The Mystical Theology of the Eastern Church,* St. Vladimir's Seminary Press, Crestwood, NY 10707, 1976, p. 205.

(26) *Op. Cit.,* Kadloubovsky, p. 248.

(27) *Op. Cit.,* Luibheid, p. 137.

(28) *Ibid.,* pps. 138-9.

(29) *Op. Cit.,* Nicodemus, p. 237.

(30) Weatherhead, Leslie D., *The Will of God,* Festival Books, Abingdon Press, Nashville, 1976, p. 31.

(31) *Op. Cit.,* Lossky, p. 205.

(32) *Op. Cit.,* Luibheid, p. 146.

(33) *Ibid.,* p. 146.

(34) *Op. Cit.,* Leech, p. 137.

(35) *The Methodist Hymnal,* Board of Publications of the United Methodist Church, Nashville, 1964, #152.

(36) *Op. Cit.,* Gillet, p. 70.

(37) *Ibid.,* p. 29, See Contra Celsum I, 67.

(38) *Op. Cit.,* Brianchaninov, p. 80.

(39) *Op. Cit.,* Kudloubovsky, pps. 308-9.

(40) *Op. Cit.,* Underhill, *The Spiritual Life,* pps. 83-5.

(41) *Ibid.*, p. 85.

(42) *Ibid.*, pps. 88-9.

(43) *Ibid.*, pps. 99-100.

(44) Tillich, Paul, *The Shaking of the Foundations,* New York, Charles Scribner's Sons, 1948, p. 155.

(45) *Op. Cit.*, Mendelson, p. 352.

(46) *Op. Cit.*, Tillich, pps. 161-2.

(47) *Op. Cit.*, Lossky, p. 202.

(48) *Op. Cit.*, Kudloubovsky, p. 249.

(49) *Ibid.*, p. 281.

(50) *Op. Cit.*, Lossky, p. 199.

(51) Sugden, E.H., *The Standard Sermons of John Wesley: Vol. 1,* London: The Epworth Press, 1966, p. 143.

(52) *Op. Cit.*, *The Methodist Hymnal,* #279.

(53) *Op. Cit.*, Lossky, p. 207.

(54) *Ibid.*, p. 199.

(55) *Ibid.*, p. 214.

(56) *Op. Cit.*, Sugden, Footnote 5 (Sermon LXXXV, iii., 4), p. 141.

(57) Helms, Hal M., (Trans.), *The Confessions of St. Augustine,* Paraclete Press, 1966, p. 7.

(58) *Op. Cit.*, Nicodemus, p. 172.

(59) *Ibid.*, p. 229.

(60) *Op. Cit.*, Lossky, p. 204.

(61) *Op. Cit.*, Underhill, *The Spiritual Life,* pps. 56-7.

(62) *Op. Cit.*, Nicodemus, pps. 201-2.

(63) *Op. Cit.*, Garvey, p. 70.

(64) *Op. Cit.*, Gillet, p. 70.

(65) *Op. Cit.*, Luibheid, p. 131.

(66) *Op. Cit.*, Brianchaninov, p. 112.

(67) *The Book of Worship for Church and Home,* The United Methodist Publishing House, Nashville, 1964, p. 386.

(68) Thielicke, Helmut (H. George Anderson, Trans.), *Being a Christian When the Chips Are Down,* Fortress Press and William Collins Sons & Co., Ltd., London, 1979, p. 64.

(69) *Op. Cit.*, Bloom, *Beginning to Pray,* p. 45.

(70) *Op. Cit.*, Kadloubovsky, p. 158.

(71) Bloom, Anthony, *Living Prayer,* Templegate Publishers, Springfield, IL 62705, 1966, p. 110.

(72) *Ibid.*, p. 110.

(73) *Op. Cit.*, Lossky, p. 209.

(74) *Ibid.*, p. 209.

(75) *Ibid.*, p. 208.

(76) *Op. Cit.*, Gillet, p. 109.

(77) *Ibid.*, p. 109.

(78) *Op. Cit.*, Lossky, pps. 212-3.

(79) *Op. Cit.*, Barclay, p. 109.

(80) *Op. Cit.*, *The Methodist Hymnal*, #289.

(81) Solzhenitsyn, Alexander, *Stories and Prose Poems*, Farrar, Staus and Giroux, 19 Union Square West, New York, NY 10003, 1971, p. 52.

(82) *Op. Cit.*, Luibheid, p. 196.

(83) *Op. Cit.*, *The Methodist Hymnal*, #251.

(84) *Richard Rodgers, Oscar Hammerstein, 1951.*

(85) *Op. Cit.*, Garvey, p. 43.

(86) *Ibid.*, p. 45.

(87) *Ibid.*, p. 45.

(88) *Op. Cit.*, Luibheid, p. 229.

(89) *Op. Cit.*, Garvey, p. 45.

(90) *Ibid.*, pps. 47-8.

(91) *Ibid.*, p. 92.

(92) *Op. Cit.*, Luibheid, p. 289.

(93) *Op. Cit.*, Garvey, p. 51.

(94) *Ibid.*, p. 49.

(95) *Ibid.*, p. 52., as quoted from Dostoevsky's *The Brothers Karamazov*.

(96) *Op. Cit.*, Garvey, p. 105.

(97) *Ibid.*, p. 103.

(98) *Op. Cit.*, Kadloubovsky, p. 190.

(99) *Op. Cit.*, Garvey, p. 101.

(100) *Ibid.*, p. 102.

(101) Bonhoeffer, Dietrich, *The Cost of Discipleship*, The Macmillan Company, Macmillan Paperback Edition, 1963, p. 127.

(102) *Ibid.*, p. 21.

(103) *Op. Cit.*, Underhill, *The Spiritual Life*, p. 113.

PRAYER AND ICONS

We live increasingly in a world where overstimulation is an undeniable fact of life. Henri Nouwen describes this world in the introduction to his valuable book, *Praying with Icons:* "Posters, billboards, television, videocassettes, movies..continuously assault our eyes and inscribe their images upon our memories."(1) We do have other choices than the usual one wherein we passively consent to be victim to the purveyors of this world's goods. One obvious alternative is to pull the plug! Another is to become intent on the visual element in our lives, and to begin to see it as a gate to that invisible realm within us which is the abode of God.

One way to do this is through the use of icons in prayer, a suggestion that may seem astonishing to those who were not reared in the Eastern Orthodox tradition. Such a suggestion seems to suggest a retreat from the world, and even if such a retreat were possible, the prospect does not seem entirely responsible. Many Christians who are committed to social action in the world argue that the world needs sensitive and spiritually aware men and women to contribute a humane aspect to its social structure, rather than embrace an otherworldliness that the use of icons seems to suggest. Who will redeem the world if we are off somewhere praying with icons?

Actually, this concern would be valid were it not for the fact that icons have the power to move us beyond the image to an encounter with the reality that the image expresses. The icon is a point of departure. It becomes the place where we gather up all we know about the nature of God, or Christ, or the saint whose life we would begin to emulate. It becomes the place where meditation can begin.

Metropolitan Anthony tells us what we must do before the icon: "What we must do is collect all the knowledge of God which we possess in order to come into His presence, but then remember that all we know about God is our past, as it were, behind our back, and we are standing face to face with God in all His complexity, all His simplicity, so close and yet unknown. Only if we stand completely open before the unknown, can the unknown reveal itself, Himself, as He chooses to reveal Himself to us as we are today. So with this open-heartedness and open-mindedness, we must stand before God without trying to give Him a shape or to imprison Him in concepts and images, and we must knock at the door.''(2)

To meditate before an icon as a prelude to prayer, far from being a retreat from the world, may actually mean beginning to participate in its redemption with a focus and energy that heretofore may have eluded us. The icon would lead us to the world of the Spirit where we may experience the transforming power of grace. This grace energizes us to participate in the redemption of the world through its transformation in love.

There is a growing interest in the icon as art, especially now as changes in the Soviet Union and Eastern Europe continue to make these societies less remote. We should be warned at the outset, however that the icon is not merely a type of collectible art. Many who are initially drawn to the icon as "art" discover that it is not art at all but a window to heaven, as it claims to be! This is an unsettling discovery, even for men and women of faith. Apart from faith, such a discovery can be devastating! The icon is a vehicle to spiritual reality, and those who play with spiritual realities play with fire!

At the core of the theology that gave birth to the icon is the conviction that through the Incarnation, God became man that man might become God. This theology claims that the Holy Spirit works within us, not merely to edify us, but to deify us, and through us, the whole Creation. The icon with its otherworldly mien is undergirded by a theology which affirms the essential goodness of this world, and the conviction that this world is capable of movement toward the light through grace.

This belief, first articulated by St. John of Damascus, holds that in Christ we share the image of God. This image was neither completely effaced by the Fall, nor by the corporate history of the world, nor by our own history of pride and self-will. The saint saw Genesis 2:26 as a paradigm for this movement toward the light: "Let us make man in our own image, after our likeness." Orthodox theology makes a distinction between "image" and "likeness." "Image" refers to that

free-will which all humans share and which resembles that free-will with which God acts. "Likeness," signifies the acquisition of grace through struggle. Diadochus the Blessed says:
"This image is given to him in his spirit and his free will. But the image must be revealed in the likeness and this is accomplished in freedom and in the gift of the self in love. The likeness to God is realized by effort and sacrifice; it is fulfilled by grace, but not without the freedom of man...for the mark of the seal can only be imprinted on the wax if it is molten."(3)
The image of God is ineffaceable in man, but the likeness of God is not. It can only increase or decrease so as to be lost altogether.(4)
In the painting—or writing—of an icon, we see a paradigm for this movement toward the Light of God. As the iconographer establishes the basic outline through the tracing, so at baptism, the grace of God begins to trace in us the outline of the image of God. As the iconographer fills-in the outline with the darker colors and models the distinctive features of the saint through the use of lighteners, so we move toward the Light—the likeness of God—through obedience.(5)
"Henceforth," observes Leonid Ouspensky, "by following Christ, by integrating himself in His body, man can re-establish in himself the divine likeness and make it shine forth in the universe. In the words of St. Paul, '..we all, with unveiled faces, beholding the glory of the Lord, are being changed into His likeness from one degree into another.' "(6)
In light of this background, let it suffice to say that our approach to the icon requires long and prayerful attention. Some degree of familiarity with the life of the saint depicted is essential. If the icon depicts an event recorded in scripture of the life of the church, it is helpful to enter into that event through the imagination. In the icon of Christ's triumphal entry into Jerusalem, I try to imagine myself as one of the children laying garments on the road, or in a tree, cutting branches. I try to imagine myself as one of the disciples, and then one of the Sadducees intent on protecting his social privileges.
To simply study an icon will not do. One must meditate upon it, and this means becoming centered on its inner stillness, purging the mind of random thoughts, and becoming collected and attentive. This is a daunting task which might well be compared to attempting to catch a butterfly with a bulldozer. Persistence is the key, and it is well worth the effort. The icon of St. Nicholas expresses the goal of meditation.

Figure 2

(Figure 2) His features convey a profound sense of energy and discipline held in creative tension. This is a state that we must strive to enter, and enter it we may only as our prayer and purification responds to divine grace.(7)

The work of the icon is to help us focus our attention through meditation to the point where a state of prayer is possible. The goal of the icon in this regard is, according to John Baggley, "..neither to provoke nor to exalt a natural human feeling, (but to) orient all of our feelings as well as our intellect towards the transfiguration, stripping them of all emotional exaltation."(8) This inner stillness, attentiveness and recollection invites us to participate in the saint's pilgrimage,(9) while looking to Jesus, who is the pioneer and perfector of our faith. (Hebrews 12:2)

Each detail in the icon has been assigned a precise meaning. The icon, like the Word itself, contains nothing peripheral or non-essential to its life. The frame, itself an integral part of the icon, emphasizes the conviction that the icon is a window to eternity, and to pass beyond the frame is to enter a reality where neither the canons of human logic nor the rules of space and time abide. Although the icon depicts an event in time, it is an event which transcends time, for it repeats itself within the deepest self once collectedness and attentiveness is achieved. St. Macarius the Great says:

"Doors are opened...and man enters the interior of many abodes; and as he enters, still other doors are opened before him, and he is enriched; and to the degree that he is enriched, new marvels are shown to him."(10)

To Western eyes, there are two canons of composition of which the iconographer seems ignorant. These are perspective, and consistency relative to the depiction of light and shadow. By ignoring these conventions, however, the iconographer is telling us that in Eternity the rules of space and time no longer apply. Uncreated light comes from within, and casts no shadow. Many would dismiss the icon as primitive art, but the icon is neither primitive, nor is it "art"!

According to the rules of optics, the lines of perspective recede from the viewer and converge at the horizon. The dimensions of objects decrease with distance which gives the illusion of depth. This use of perspective is easily diagramed in a work such as Da Vinci's *Last Supper.* Ouspensky suggests that what we have here is essentially an optical illusion which fascinates the spectator into a futile game of appearances.(11)

In the icon, there is a type of perspective which is called an "inverse" perspective. Whereas in a Western painting, the background figures are reduced in size to create an illusion of depth, the background figures in an icon may be slightly larger than the figures in the foreground. This, in effect, reverses the lines of perspective. As a consequence, they converge, not at the horizon line, but before the person viewing the icon. Thus the frame of the icon is the narrow gate that leads to life. (Figure 3)

"Once embarked on the path to which the gate leads," Ouspensky suggests, "man sees endless possibilities and perspectives opening before him, and this path, far from becoming narrow, becomes wider. But in the beginning, it is but a simple point in our hearts, from which our whole perspective must be reversed. This is the authentic and literal meaning of the word *metanoia,* which means 'reversal of the intellect.' "(12)

The icon ignores the rules of composition relative to reproducing the light and shade that would occur in nature, because the source of light is the icon itself. The luminescent quality of the icon comes partly from the gold ground, and partly from the faces of the saints. The radiance of the faces correspond to the Biblical description of the sanctified state of man: Moses as he descended from the mountain, and Stephen in his martyrdom. It is this luminous character which gives the icon its soul. As Egon Sendler has observed:

"In the icon we see a divine reality which at the same time respects this earthly world because it is created by God to become transfigured in his Spirit. If the representation loses the character of God's mystery, if it reduces this mystery to the sensible forms of matter the icon loses its soul."(13)

The light of the icon coalesces within the halo. This is a device which expresses the radiance of the saints which cannot be seen save through the eyes of faith.

In addition to what first appears as ignorance of the canons of perspective and light and dark, the architectural forms which appear in the icon are fanciful and ignore the law of gravity. Columns neither appear capable of supporting their own weight nor of fulfilling their customary function. Doors and windows are placed haphazardly and appear to be entirely non-functional. But here again is expressed a

Figure 3

spiritual truth: the foolishness of God is wiser than human wisdom and the weakness of God stronger than human strength. The architecture of the icon for all its whimsy, is never anything more than a background device. It never encloses, for that would limit access to the event being depicted.

The most compelling aspect of the icon is the face of the Holy. The Orthodox hold that descriptions of the saints were at first transmitted by oral tradition or by actual portraits. These earliest representations—called prototypes—have disappeared, but have been lovingly and faithfully reproduced throughout the ages. The iconographer becomes familiar not only with existing representations, but with descriptions of the prototypes found in the painters' manuals.(14) The traits of the face, hair and wrinkles are all faithfully reproduced, but with an eye to divesting the image of all sensuality. The non-naturalistic manner of depicting the sense organs, the eyes without brilliance, the ears strangely shaped, "conveys deafness, detachment from all excitation and, conversely, the receptiveness of the spiritual world by those who have attained holiness."(15) The face and eyes, which perhaps best express the spiritual life of the person, convey the power of the Spirit over the body.(16) The "look" of the icon is devoid of all physical heaviness, for the saint has purified his or her life by fasting and vigils, thus the face is full of peace and serenity. Nicephorus Blemmydes has left us these words: "We were not born to eat or drink but to shine by our virtues in the glory of our creator. We eat out of necessity so as to preserve our strength for contemplation for which we were really born."(17) The forehead of the saint is high and is identified as the seat of wisdom. Its rising above the arches of the eyes tends to strengthen the intensity of the gaze. The nose has its roots at the base of the forehead and is elongated to give an expression of nobility. The nostrils betray no heaviness and seem to "vibrate with the movement of the Spirit, thus expressing the saint's passion for God..(18) The mouth, often the most sensual part of the face, is usually very thin and is always closed in contemplation."(19)

The face of the icon speaks more powerfully than words. Like any living symbol, it bypasses the intellect and enters into the deepest self. Kenneth Leech says in this regard:

"This is the essence of worship, and this is why we should never expect to 'understand' everything we do, capture it all in our heads. In worship we are entering into the mystery of the universe, the mystery of the infinite and eternal God. If we catch something of that splendour beyond words, we have made some progress."(20)

Those called to be iconographers are given the task of translating this inner sanctification into images. The Orthodox regard the actual writing of an icon as an act of worship. The inconographer prays, fasts and meditates in order to write an icon, and looks upon the role as a religious vocation.(21) The materials of the iconographer include representatives of the animal, vegetable and mineral realms. These fundamental materials, which include water, chalk, glue, pigments and egg yolk, are products of God's good world. These the inconographer purifies and consecrates to God.(22) The process of creating an icon is itself a sign of the Incarnation, in which God appeared through matter to redeem the material world.

The icon invites the beholder to enter into the mysterious world of the deepest self. As part of our entry into this mysterious world, we are called to work with the Holy Spirit that our likeness to God may be fashioned through His grace and our response.

(1) Nouwen, Henri, J.M., *Behold The Beauty of the Lord: Praying with Icons,* Ave Maria Press, Notre Dame, Indiana, 1987, p. 12.

(2) Bloom, Anthony, *Beginning to Pray,* Paulist Press, New York/Ramsey, N.J., 1970, p. 45.

(3) Ouspensky, Leonid, *Theology of the Icon,* St. Vladimir's Seminary Press, Crestwood, NY 10707, 1978, p. 185.

(4) *Ibid.,* p. 188.

(5) *Ibid.,* p. 185.

(6) *Ibid.,* p. 188.

(7) Baggley, John, *Doors of Perception—Icons and Their Spiritual Significance,* St. Vladimir's Seminary Press, Crestwood, NY 10707, 1988, p. 80.

(8) *Op. Cit.,* Ouspensky, p. 211.

(9) *Op. Cit.,* Baggley, p. 80.

(10) *Op. Cit.,* Ouspensky, p. 225.

(11) *Ibid.,* p. 225.

(12) *Ibid.,* p. 225.

(13) Sendler, Egon, *The Icon: Image of the Invisible,* Oakwood Publications, 616 Knob Hill Ave, Redondo Beach, CA 90277, p. 182.

(14) *Ibid.,* p. 61.

(15) *Op. Cit.,* Ouspensky, p. 208.

(16) *Ibid.,* p. 209.

(17) *Op. Cit.,* Sendler, p. 58.

(18) *Ibid.*, p. 64.

(19) *Ibid.*, p. 64.

(20) Leech, Kenneth, *True Prayer: An Invitation to Christian Spirituality,* Harper & Row Publishers Inc., 10 East 53rd St., New York, NY 10022, pps. 112-3.

(21) Underhill, Evelyn, *Worship,* Crossroad, New York, 1989, p. 39.

(22) Ouspensky, Leonid and Lossky, Vladimir, *The Meaning of Icons,* St. Vladimir's Seminary Press, Crestwood, NY, 1982, p. 54.

CORPORATE PRAYER

THE LORD'S PRAYER

OUR FATHER, WHO ART IN HEAVEN

The Lord's Prayer is the one prayer that almost every Christian knows by heart. It is a prayer that begins and ends with the praise of God. Individual petitions are ranked below the praise of His name, His coming Kingdom and the holiness of His will. In every line there is the call for the submission of our wills to His. Thus, it is not only a prayer, but "a whole way of life expressed in the form of a prayer."(1) Its goal, as is the case of every true prayer, is God Himself. Yet how quickly we recite it! Leonard Foley OFM reminds us that this is the Lord's Prayer, and "he delights to hear us say it. Slowly."(2) St. Ignatius Loyola once observed in this same spirit that one who prays this prayer should say "Father," and then "reflect upon this word as long as he finds meaning, comparisons, relish and consolation in the consideration of it. He should then continue the same method with each word..."(3)

Helmut Thielicke observes that prayer—especially this prayer— must be spoken as we might speak to our earthly father. "When speaking with your father you don't look in a mirror; you direct your gaze toward him."(4) Yet, we must not seek to make God in our own image. He is infinitely pure, calm and holy, and thus beyond our imagining. He is as this first phrase of the prayer reminds us, in heaven. This means that He is infinitely more remote than the nearest star, and yet so intimately involved in His creation that not one sparrow falls to the ground without His knowing. (Matt. 10:29)

One aspect of the mystery of the Incarnation is the revelation that by grace we are brothers and sisters of Jesus and in Jesus, and also each to the other. Yet none of these things are so unless they become so for us. It is only through Christ that our eyes are opened and we become self-conscious sons and daughters of God.

When Jesus teaches us that God is our Father, this is truly a new thing (Jer. 31:22), for although God is spoken of as Father fourteen times in the Old Testament, in every instance the reference is to Israel as His firstborn. No one in Judaism ever addressed God as "my Father." Yet, this is precisely what Jesus does in his prayers, and this some twenty-one times. In all, Jesus refers to God as His Father one hundred and seventy times. Only in His cry of dereliction from the cross is "my father" missing.

Although the Greek text of the Gospels indicated this only once (Mark 14:36), there is every likelihood that Jesus was accustomed to referring to His Father as "Abba." No doubt this alone would have offended the pharisees, because "Abba" is equivalent to the English word "Daddy." Clearly, Jesus was not indulging in infantilism, as would be the case if our adult children were accustomed to calling us "mommy" or "daddy." He does this to encourage a childlike relationship to God on the part of believers. He says also "...anyone who does not welcome the Kingdom of God like a little child will never enter it." (Luke 18:17)

We learn from Paul's letters that the early church came to share in Jesus's own intimate relationship with God. In Romans 8:15, for example, Paul expresses this relationship using Jesus's own affectionate word. "The spirit you received was not the spirit of slaves bringing fear into your lives again; it is the spirit of sons and it makes us cry out, Abba, Father."

This relationship from God's side will never be broken, as Metropolitan Anthony observes:

"...when the prodigal son returned to his father and was about to say: 'I am no more worthy to be called thy son, make me as one of thy hired servants!' (Luke 15:19), the father allowed him to pronounce the first words: 'I have sinned against heaven and in thy sight and am no more worthy to be called thy son,' but there he stopped him. Yes, he is not worthy, but he is a son in spite of his unworthiness. You cannot cease to be a member of your family whatever you do, worthy or not."(5)

We live in an age that is sensitive to "inclusive" language, and many ask, "Why not 'Our Mother'?" God is compared to a mother by Isaiah, who says, "Like a son comforted by his mother I (God) will comfort you." (66:13) Human beings, male and female, are made in the image of God. (Gen. 1:26-7; 5:1-2) Jesus compares himself to a mother hen in Matthew's Gospel (23:37) and John likens the resurrection to a woman in labor. (16:21)

John Killinger says, however, that the role of the mother, while unique, is different from that of the father. A mother's relationship to her child is organic. She "carries the child in the womb, nurtures it there, bears it, and nurtures it again."(6) The relationship of the father to the child, on the other hand, is primarily psychological, a relationship Killinger calls that of the "intimate outsider."(7) The critical importance of the child's relationship to this "intimate outsider" he continues, is revealed in the story of the conflict between Jacob and Esau, and the blessing that only their father Isaac could bestow.

When I was a divinity student, I worked for a time at a church in Washington D.C.'s inner city. The children and young people with whom I worked came mostly from one-parent families. In virtually every situation, the mother was the parent who provided the home and who was the primary care-giver. Many of these women worked long, exhausting hours outside the home and to their credit still managed to fulfill many of their children's emotional needs. I still don't understand how many of them managed. Yet the children looked to the male members of our team to provide some "blessing" in their lives. Often we found ourselves overwhelmed by their demands for attention and approval. Every gesture of interest, every encouraging word, they devoured as though they were eating their last meal. The female members of the staff had these demands laid upon them as well, but we males seemed to have some special, indefinable role. I realize now that we were "father figures" to these kids, and I hope that we were able to fulfill that role, if only in a small way.

Part of the mystery of the Incarnation is that even if we lack an earthly father, we still have a Heavenly Father, and Jesus invites us to address Him with the familiar terms of childhood.

The Lord's Prayer, however, begins with a word we must not overlook, and that is the pronoun "Our." This tells us that we are not "only children" but part of the fellowship of all who believe and pray. We are informed by this very first word that sibling rivalry finds no quarter within the Kingdom of God. There is no private way to the Father that ignores the fact that we have brothers and sisters.

When we were growing up, there was no way we could draw our parents into taking sides in our squabbles. They were unflinchingly impartial and forever reconciling. Even today, if I have had words with my brother, or ignored one of my sisters' birthdays, I can expect to receive a discreet note from my folks.

The Lord's Prayer is like one of these notes. It reminds us at the outset that we are part of a family, the wholeness of which depends in part upon our good will. As Kenneth Leech has indicated, there is a point beneath the words where we must meet as children in the presence of our Father.(8) This meeting validates and vivifies our individual prayers, which are given wings by the Holy Spirit. This is what Jesus meant when He said, "Where two or three are gathered in my name, there am I in their midst." (Matt. 18:19-20) The essential corporateness of God's family and of the Lord's Prayer itself is reaffirmed by St. Cyprian, who says:

"(Father)..is a title none of us would dare appropriate in prayer had He Himself not allowed us to. And so, dear friends, since we call God our Father, let us remember to act like children of God, so that He may find pleasure in having us as His children, just as we do in having Him as our Father."(9)

HALLOWED BE THY NAME

Jesus has taught us a new name for God; a name appropriate for the use of those who have entered the kingdom as little children. It is a name that expresses unqualified trust, and a profound faith in God's providential care. The name "Abba" would seem an affront to the majesty of the Father had not He Himself revealed it to us through the Incarnation of His Son, and allowed us to become His sons and daughters.

This does not mean that God has been "unmasked," like some taciturn history professor who holds his class in thrall until the day his infant child bursts into the room and turns the practiced scowl into a smile. It does not mean that God has been "exposed," as when the little dog Toto brought down the Wizard of Oz by drawing aside the curtain. The Incarnation does not compromise the majesty of God. His holiness is in no way diminished. It is, rather, made accessible to us.

We are not asking that God be made holy by our prayers. Rather, as St. Cyprian says, we are "begging from God that His name be hallowed in us."(10) We hallow God's name by letting His holiness be seen in our lives, and this is accomplished when people discover that there is more to our being than that which disciplined living might produce. We hallow God's name when we glow with the fire of divine love.

"Hallowed be thy name" is our plea that we might continue in our ascent to God. Once we were slaves who obeyed out of fear, then hirelings who obeyed for the sake of reward. Now, we would be sons and daughters who act out of love. This is a prayer that what has been kindled in our lives by the Spirit may continue to burn, and that we may persevere in what we have already begun to be.(11)

We seem in our time, to have mislaid the idea of the Holy. This was brought home to me several years ago during a conversation with a man with whom I had worked closely in YMCA committee work. I had offered my church as a meeting place and he, arriving early, said, "This place even smells like a church!" To my question, "What does a church smell like?" he had a ready answer. "It is the smell of old attics and museums, of libraries and school buildings in the summer. You know what I mean! It's the musty odor of sanctity!"

He was not speaking for himself, but for the age! So this is what the Holy—or rather, our idea of the Holy—has become? How this has changed since the early days of the church. Then, St. John Climacus said that the Holy should inspire "the fear we have in the presence of rulers and wild beasts."(12)

Perhaps we have tried to domesticate the Holy with our collective intellect. Detreich Bonhoeffer perceived the problem well when he wrote:

"..Christians are talking where they should be listening. He who can no longer listen to his brother will soon be no longer listening to God either: he will be doing nothing but prattle in the presence of God too. This is the beginning of the death of the Spiritual life, and in the end there is nothing left."(13)

Perhaps this dread day is already upon us, for, as Leech suggests: "There has been a decay of symbols...there is a loss of wonder. So much in our society is artificial. There is even a center in the United States where non-holiday makers can have their photographs taken outside reconstructions of overseas places of interest which they haven't visited. The effect of the cult of the artificial in spiritual life is seen in the fact that all too often there is a kind of lifelessness and immobility about 'religious' people, a failure to be quite alive. Why? Because the concept of God, which was originally rooted in a vital experience, has become mere lifeless jargon which corresponds to nothing in their experience."(14)

Have we tried to subdue the Holy with our talk? Jacob wrestled with an angel in the attempt to subdue a mystery, but the angel didn't even reveal his name, and before the battle was over, Jacob was hobbled for life. Even Moses tried, in a way, to domesticate the mystery which called from the center of the burning bush. Like Jacob, he demanded, "What is your name?" But this time there was an answer, and it was "Yahweh—I am who I am. I am He who is! I am not begotten! Take off your shoes! The place upon which you stand is holy ground!"

There was no odor that day of musty attics and museums! This was divine incandescence and this Moses would communicate to the Hebrew children, who ever after forbade mention of the divine name. For, as John Killinger has suggested, "to say the name of the real God was like releasing the power of a thousand thunderstorms at once, therefore the name Yahweh, the most powerful of all the names of God, was spoken only once a year, and by the High Priest when he entered the Holy of Holies in the Temple."(15)

The holiness of God, which we pray will be revealed in us, is linked to His glory, the radiant power of His being. As such it involves the idea of "to be terrible," and "to shine brightly."(16) The holiness of God causes things to become holy through proximity to Him. The ground upon which Moses stands becomes holy because of its nearness to God and its use by Him. (Ex. 3:5; Josh. 5:15) This is true also of the Ark of the Covenant (2 Chron. 35:3), the Sabbath (Ex. 20:8-11), and the saints through whom His name is hallowed.

Isaiah's response to this holiness is what we might call a holy terror, for he says, "Woe is me! For I am lost!" His lips are seared by the divine fire, for he will become a living sacrifice. In the midst of the cry of one entirely undone, he is cleansed, purged, and commissioned in a type of baptism.

Christians are called to be holy, and this involves movement from the state of being outside the gate to that of son or daughter. Yet holiness is never our doing. If it is found within us, its purpose is to reveal something of the nature of God—His joy, His love, and His peace.

To pray, "Hallowed be thy name," is to submit to the divine will. As C.S. Lewis has observed, "..God wills our good and our good is to love Him and to love Him we must know Him: and if we would know Him, we shall in fact fall on our faces...Yet the call is not only to prostration and awe; it is to a reflection of the divine life, a creaturely participation in the Divine attributes which is far beyond our present desires. We are bidden to 'put on Christ,' to become like God!"(17)

A life of prayer cannot but lead to growth in holiness and participation in this intense, blazing love. As Isaiah discovered, this growth involves burning; the sacrifice which is pain and anguish of spirit. This is the way of the Cross, and it leads inevitably through deprivation and inner suffering. Leech tells us that this way of the cross involves a confrontation with self, a stripping away of the false self, a purifying of the personality.(18) It is through the way of the cross that the name of God is hallowed in us.

Again, St. Cyprian has the last word: "But because He Himself said, be Holy, for I am Holy (Lv. 20:7) we beg that we who have been sanctified through baptism may persevere in what we have begun to be."(19)

THY KINGDOM COME, THY WILL BE DONE
ON EARTH AS IT IS IN HEAVEN

When we pray "thy kingdom come, thy will be done on earth as it is in heaven," we are asking two things: that God's Kingdom be made present *to* us and that it be made present *in* us. We are praying that the Creation be restored to a perfect reflection of His will, and that we become fit for this Kingdom. We are praying for a deep transformation within, that we might share the divine nature. (2 Pet. 1:4)

When we pray "Thy Kingdom come," we pray that we might become one in solidarity with God in the spirit of His Kingdom. As St. Cyprian puts it:

"What we are praying for is the coming of *our* kingdom—the one promised us by God and gained by Christ's bloody passion—that having first served him on earth we may begin to reign with him as Lord..."(20)

Every prayer which is a surrender to the will of God becomes a Kingdom-centered prayer. A Kingdom-centered prayer invites the Holy Spirit to kindle within us the passion to accept His will and the grace to do it. The great George Croly hymn text is actually a prayer in this same spirit:

Teach me to love thee as thine angels love,
One holy passion filling all my frame;
the kindling of the heaven descended dove,
My heart an altar and my love the flame.(21)

When we pray in this spirit we must be ready to pay whatever price may be required of us. For then, as Metropolitan Anthony says: "...we say in a new way, Thy will be done; not as an alien will, but as a will with which we have become completely harmonious. And we must, at the moment we do this, accept all that is implied in being sons of God, in being members of the one body. As he came into the world, so are we elect for this purpose; and it may be at the cost of our own lives that we are to bring peace around us and establish the kingdom."(22)

The Kingdom is not merely what might be described as an interior spiritual presence, although it certainly includes that aspect. Neither is it of a wholly different order, although when it dawns in its fullness, its every part will appear different.

The Kingdom for which we pray is nothing less than the transformation of Creation: rocks and trees, birds and beasts, human beings, the face of the earth, and the universe.

It is a vision of the future of God, but the vision is not wholly of the future. It is a vision of Eternity, but it has its beginnings in time. It is entirely a gift of God, which will reach fruition when He chooses, but we who believe on His name may begin to effect it now through faith. It is this participation to which the prophet Isaiah refers when he claims his vocation:

"The spirit of the Lord Yahweh has been given to me, for Yahweh has anointed me. He has sent me to bring good news to the poor, to bind up hearts that are broken; to proclaim liberty to the captives, freedom to those in prison." (61:1-2)

In the vision of the prophet Micah, the Kingdom unfolds in time, bringing peace among the nations and the liberation of individuals. The Lord Yahweh will wield His authority over the many peoples and arbitrate for the nations. They will beat their swords into plow-shares and their spears into pruning hooks. Each man will sit under his own vine and fig tree and there will be no one to trouble him. (4:3-4)

102

The Kingdom clause in the Lord's Prayer reflects the Kiddush prayer of the synagogue, a prayer our Lord knew by heart:

"Magnified and sanctified be His great name in the world which He has created according to His will. May He establish His Kingdom in your lifetime, and in your days, and in the lifetime of the House of Israel, even speedily and at a near time."

The words of the prophets and the hope of the Jews is visible to us in the Incarnation. He is the Word made flesh. (John 1:14) He who took flesh is true God. Had this not been so, our salvation could not have occurred. Our prayer "Thy Kingdom come" is founded upon our relationship with the God who emptied Himself, assumed the condition as a slave and became one like us. (Phil. 2:7) It is through this flesh that our salvation comes.(23)

The Kingdom clause reflects our faith that in the Incarnation salvation is already taking place and evil is already under siege. This is the meaning of Luke 10:18-19 where Jesus says that he saw Satan falling like lightning from heaven, and that because of this nothing shall hurt the disciples. In fact, they shall have power to tread serpents and scorpions underfoot as well as the whole strength of the enemy.

From these words we conclude that the Kingdom is both "already" and "not yet." He sends word to John in prison that the Kingdom is already. The blind receive their sight. The lame walk. Lepers are cleansed. The deaf hear. The dead are raised and the poor have the good news preached to them. (Matt. 11:45) The Kingdom is already come for the poor in spirit, for theirs is the Kingdom of Heaven. It is already come for Zacchaeus, for today salvation is come to his house. The Kingdom is already come for the Evangelist, who recalls Jesus's words, "Whoever listens to these words of mine and believes in the One who sent me, already has eternal life." (John 5:24)

But Jesus also tells us that the Kingdom is not yet, because when it fully comes, there will be judgment. Those who treated the least, the last and the lost with compassion will be welcomed, while those who did not will be denied entry. (Matt. 25:31-40) The newly planted wheat is not yet ready for the harvest. (Matt. 13:24) The contents of the dragnet will not be sorted until the end of the day. (Matt. 13:47)

Although the final battle has not been joined, the outcome is sure. The Kingdom has already established a beachhead in our hearts and in our world. One of Winston Churchill's famous phrases is applicable here: "This is not the end, nor is it the beginning of the end, but it is the end of the beginning." Paul uses this beachhead motif when he tells the Philippians that they are a colony of heaven. (Phil. 3:20) In the meantime, we are a people whose mother city is heaven and who are on earth to "conquer it for God and bring the Kingdom of God if only to a small spot."(24)

The paradox of the Kingdom is that it is a gift of God, and that it comes to fruition only when He wills it. Yet, the will of human-kind is essential to its completion. For me, the first part of the paradox is best expressed in this doggerel:

Sit down O men of God,
His Kingdom He will bring
Whenever it may please his grace!
You cannot do a thing.(25)

The second part of the paradox is perhaps best expressed by St. Macarius, who said: "The will of man is the essential condition, for without it God does nothing."

When I was a young man I hitchhiked with a friend through Western Canada. We quickly learned that the province of Alberta was not entirely hospitable to hitchhikers. As a consequence, we spent most of one day with our thumbs in the air. Finally, when it appeared that nobody was going to give us a ride, my friend declared, "I'm tired of standing here. Let's walk!" I tried to reason with him, saying, "The nearest town is fifty miles away!" He rejoined, "You can stay there if you want, but I'm tired of sitting around here doing nothing!"

God will usher in the Kingdom when He wills it, but in the meantime, if we would be fit for it, we must do something. Thomas Merton tells us, "the greatest saints in heaven are those who can give God the most love there. Those who can give Him the most love are those who know Him best. And those who know Him best are those who have loved Him on earth."(26) Those who have loved Him best on earth, we might add, are those who have cared best for His creation.

When we pray "Thy Kingdom come," we pray that it may be fulfilled in us this day and every day; and we pray that it be fulfilled once and for all. A perfect prayer, Leonard Foley tells us, would want the latter—"God's total and perfect glorification—the end, the fulfillment, the destruction of all evil, the perfect adoration of God by his people, now (and) once and for all."(27)

GIVE US THIS DAY OUR DAILY BREAD

Leonard Foley has given a familiar Gospel story a different twist. It is the one about the distraught father who travels many miles to find Jesus, and to beg him to come and cure his daughter. On the way, Jesus receives the news that he need not trouble himself any longer as the child has died. Undeterred, he arrives at the house, and finds the mourners already in the midst of their lamentations. They laugh when he declares that the child is not dead, just asleep. The parents, and three disciples accompany him into the room. Taking the little girl by the hand he says, "Arise," and she does. Picture the five witnesses holding their breath. Can this actually be happening? Is she really alive, or will she fall back? Foley guesses what Jesus must have said next: "Well, are you going to stand there all day? Give her something to eat!"(28)

The One who calms the sea and raises the dead is also concerned for the stomach of a child. God is as concerned for the state of our bodies as for the state of our souls! This is why Jesus taught his disciples to pray, "Give us this day our daily bread."

On the face of it, this petition would seem to be more concerned about physical rather than spiritual hunger. Yet it was inevitable that the church should see a deeper meaning, and this meaning extends to all the other Gospel references to bread. Jesus also says that He is the bread of life, and that although everyone who ate manna in the desert eventually died, all those who eat the bread that comes down from heaven will not die. (John 6:48-50) Thus, it is impossible to pray this petition and not think of the Eucharist. St. Cyprian, however, said that these words may be taken either literally or spiritually, "because, in the divine plan, both readings are helpful for our salvation."(29) While a literal reading may seem to engage us at a less "lofty" plane than a spiritual reading, the incarnation makes it impossible for us to separate the physical from the spiritual without doing violence to both.

As at the beginning of the prayer where we say "Our Father" and not "my Father," it is no accident that here we pray "our daily bread" and not "my daily bread." Our personal religion must become a social religion if ever it is to get beyond mere spiritual self-gratification. The sin of the rich man in the story of the rich man and Lazarus (Luke 16:19-31) was not so much that he dressed in purple and fine linen and feasted magnificently every day. His sin was that the sight of the starving, scab-infested Lazarus did not make him sick to his stomach.

We soften the impact of this story when we assume that the rich man allowed Lazarus to eat his garbage, but the story does not indicate that he did. It tells us only that Lazarus longed to eat the scraps that fell from the rich man's table. This is a sordid picture of self-gratification and its ultimate end, and that end is Hell!

One of the ways some devotional books treat this petition is by asserting that we need not worry about food and its distribution, inasmuch as the Lord will provide. A study of human nature, however, cannot lead one to assume that this provision will be automatic. Consider the prodigal son. He would have willingly filled his stomach with the husks that remained on the floor of the hog yard, because no one offered him anything. (Luke 15:16)

Conrad Noel of Thaxted challenges us all to be more sympathetic to the plight of hungry people: "If the body is the Temple of God's Holy Ghost, then those who defraud men's bodies of proper nourishment and proper shelter and proper rest are robbing temples, and that is the sin of sacrilege."(30)

When the Kingdom comes to fruition, we will be judged in light of how we have served Christ in our neighbor. Centuries ago, St. John Chrysostom admonished his hearers to examine their profession of faith in light of this judgment:

"What is the use of loading Christ's table with vessels of gold if he himself is dying of hunger? First satisfy his hunger, then adorn the table with what remains. Tell me, if you saw a man in need of even the most necessary food, and if you should leave him standing there in order to set the table with vessels of gold, would he be thankful to you? Would he not rather be angry?...But consider well that this is the way you treat Christ when he goes about as a pilgrim, a homeless vagabond, and when instead of taking him in you embellish floors and walls and capitals of columns and suspend lamps from silver chains. I am not saying this to criticize the use of such ornaments...We must attend to both, but to Christ first."(31)

The Lord's Prayer teaches us to ask that our bread be given daily. The intent is that we ask only for the needs of the day—no more and no less. Certainly there is a close connection between this petition and the statement which follows in Matthew's sixth chapter:

"So do not worry; do not say, 'What are we to eat? What are we to drink? How are we to be clothed?' It is the pagans who set their hearts on these things. Your heavenly Father knows you need them all.

Set your hearts on his kingdom first, and on his righteousness, and all these things will be given to you as well. So do not worry about tomorrow: tomorrow will take care of itself. Each day has enough trouble of its own." (6:31-34)

Recovering alcoholics know that the "one day at a time" approach is essential to their success. Although many find that this approach reduces stress because it divides time into manageable portions, this is more than stress management. It is surrender to God. St. Maximos the Confessor writes of this surrender:

"If...we take this clause to mean that we should pray for the daily bread that sustains our present life, let us be careful not to overstep the bounds of the prayer, presumptuously assuming that we will live for many cycles of years and forgetting that we are mortal and that our life passes us by like a shadow; but free from anxiety let us pray for bread sufficient for one day at a time, thus showing that...we make life a rehearsal for death, in our purpose anticipating nature and, even before death comes, cutting off the soul's anxiety about bodily things."(32)

He recommends that we keep our bodies in good health, our aim being not just to live, but to live for God.(33)

The important thing here is that the gift of God's daily bread is a means whereby we gather strength to establish in the world a beach-head for the Kingdom.

A literal reading of this petition naturally leads to a spiritual reading. The Fathers interpreted it as referring to the mysterious bread of the Eucharist. Metropolitan Anthony says, in this regard, "Unless we are fed in this new way, mysteriously (because we depend now for our existence on God alone) we will not survive."(34)

God is present in the bread of the Eucharist sacramentally through the outward and visible sign that we receive through faith. This means that God communicates Himself through matter. The divine glory is received by faith through the material Creation. "It is because," as Leech puts it, "the world is sacramental that we can have the sacraments in the Christian church."(35)

I was raised on a wheat farm in the Midwest, where the rhythm of life was regulated by the Commodities Market in far-off Chicago. Eric Severeid, himself a product of the area, said of durum wheat that it found its way into every conversation. When the market was satisfactory, talk turned to the weather. When the weather was satisfactory, talk turned to wild oats. Bread was the product of all this concern, and it never occurred to me that there could be anything holy about it.

One sultry August Sunday morning, the colored glass windows of our country church were raised to reveal fields of the ripening wheat. When the minister raised the loaf and said, "This is my Body," I thought, "God is present to us in bread?" He is in it, actually in it, for it is the material Creation that He redeems. This same mysterious presence permeates the whole of Creation.

As far as the breaking of bread is concerned, Leech suggests that it is "the movement towards a life and a society which is marked not by competition and egocentricity, but by cooperation and self-transcendence."(36)

He suggests that this is a sign that the breaking-down of our ego is actually a breakthrough.(37) The rich man in the story of the rich man and Lazarus went to Hell because he never saw beyond himself and his own needs. A broken and contrite heart is always the beginning of self transcendence!

Bread recalls the Exodus, a figure for the spiritual journey from self-absorption to absorption in God. The bread of the Exodus was the manna which the Hebrews collected every morning and which sustained them in this journey. As this manna sustained the Hebrews, the Bread of Life is the necessary sustenance for our spiritual journey.

But how long must we be in the wilderness? The answer is that we must wander there until we are purged of all that encumbers us! There, eating and drinking has only one purpose, and that is to get us to the promised land.

The year I turned forty, I suppose it was vanity that drove me to compete in a multi-sport event which included a cross-country cycling race. Along a route which extended for one hundred and twelve miles, there were fifteen aid stations. We were advised to take refreshment at each one, and it never occurred to any of the participants to hoard the items that were freely given, because it was the race that mattered and not the refreshments. From the story of the Exodus we learn that in the beginning it was the eating and not the journey that occupied the children of Israel. That is perhaps why what might have been a ten-day trek took forty years!

Finally, bread reminds us of the end of the journey when we will sit down to the Eternal Banquet in the Kingdom when many will come from the East and the West, and sit with Abraham, Isaac and Jacob.

(Matt. 8:11) The eternal banquet, like the Kingdom, has a double aspect. It is already, and can be found wherever Christians meet for the breaking of bread and prayers. It is visible wherever Christians feed on Christ for the purpose of establishing the Kingdom, if only in a small spot. It is also not yet, and we shall not participate in it fully until God establishes His Kingdom fully. In the meantime, as St. Cyprian has said: "...we ask for bread—that is, Christ—to be given us every day, so that we who abide and live in him may not drift away from his body and the sanctification it brings."(38)

FORGIVE US OUR DEBTS

The next petition of the Lord's Prayer is about sin and reconciliation. By sin I do not mean individual sins, but a state of alienation from ourselves, others and God which may persuade us that individual "sins" might be appropriate. Before sin is an act, says Paul Tillich, it is a state.(39)

Sin is a state of alienation, or separation from God. Like the Incarnation, sin too is historic, having happened in time. We refer to sin and its continuing effects as the Fall. Yet, this is not to say that humankind and the creation itself are wholly depraved, for the Created retains the potential for rising again to its pristine state where the image of God is restored. This is not to diminish the effects of sin. Tillich says that this alienation "constitutes the state of everything that exists; it is a universal fact; it is the fate of every life."(40) When the Apostle Paul describes sin, he uses active verbs to indicate its sway over us: Sin "reigns" (Rom. 5:21; 6:14). Sin "enslaves" (Rom. 6:6,17,20).

Yet, Paul tells us that in Christ a new creation has begun which will reverse the effects of the Fall: "..It is certain that death reigned over everyone as a consequence of one man's fall, it is even more certain that one man, Jesus Christ, will cause everyone to reign in life who receives the free gift he does not deserve, of being made righteous. (Rom. 5:17)."

Forgiveness, Leech suggests, reverses the process of sin. This turns around the process of action, reaction and retaliation, which may describe many of our relationships. It brings about a whole new chain of relationships, in that it introduces a new and unpredictable factor into the situation.(41)

One who is truly in communion with God has the capacity to forgive. Metropolitan Anthony puts it this way: "to be led by God one must commune with this quality of God which is the ability to forgive."(42) When we are able to pray, "Forgive us our debts as we forgive our debtors," and actually live out the implications of this petition in the real world, we are not far from the Kingdom of God.

When I was a boy, I thought that the biggest difference between the Methodists and Lutherans was that we Methodists said, "trespasses," and the Lutherans in our town said "debts." Being a Methodist and, to my mind, correct, I considered that the Lutherans were just being obstinate! Yet, not even the venerable King James Version had retained the "trespasses" of Wycliffe and Tyndale. The word survived only in the traditions of common and private prayer.

"Trespass" is an entirely appropriate word, as every lad who has stolen crab apples from a neighbor's tree would agree. In Middle English it meant "to go across," or "to violate." Tillich picks up on this word when he describes the effects of sin as feeling that "we have violated another life, a life which we loved, or from which we were estranged."(43)

"Debt" is also a good word, because when we are unforgiving we are actually in debt to God. Ours is the state of the tenant who will not pay the rent, or the spendthrift who must pass bad checks to finance his or her lifestyle. In either case, someone else must pick up the tab. That "someone else" is God.

Yet, our indebtedness is, as it were, forgiven as we ourselves forgive. When we show mercy, God shines the light of His mercy upon us! Conversely, what we do not forgive, God holds against us. Everything has its price, and the price of our being unforgiving will eventually be our damnation! Metropolitan Anthony says, "It is not that God does not want to forgive, but if we become unforgiving, we check the mystery of love, we refuse it and there is no place for us in the kingdom."(44)

Perhaps we are unforgiving because we have not yet tasted forgiveness ourselves? How shall we demonstrate forgiveness if we ourselves do not know what forgiveness is? If, however, we pray for forgiveness in the faith that we shall receive it, receive it we will, and when it comes, it will look like this:

"Sometimes..a wave of light breaks into our darkness, and it is as though a voice were saying, 'You are accepted. You are accepted,

accepted by that which is greater than you, and the name of which you do not know...Do not try to do anything now; perhaps later you will do much. Do not seek anything; do not perform anything; do not intend anything. Simply accept the fact that you are accepted.' "(45)

Until we ourselves know this forgiveness and this acceptance, we shall not be able to give it to those who require it from us.

Metropolitan Anthony would remind us that what we usually call forgiveness is nothing more than probation. He points out that we wait patiently for some evidence of repentance, and want to be sure that the penitent is truly sorry for what he or she has done.(46) Leslie Weatherhead gives us an excellent example of probationary forgiveness:

"I heard of a churchgoing woman whose maid 'sinned' in giving birth to a child outside marriage. The woman 'forgave' the maid, but even years afterward rebuked the maid for some trifling fault, and said to her, 'You are not nearly grateful enough to me, Ethel; it isn't every woman who would take a fallen girl into her home.'"(47)

He says further that Ethel should not only have been forgiven but treated as righteous in the hope that forgiving love would enable her to be created anew.(48) This is what God would do for each of us. He accepts us, not for what we are, but for what we may become. This process is called Justification by Faith, and it gradually disperses a sense of guilt by the continual treating of the person as righteous.(49)

The prodigal son may have returned from the far country wasted in body, mind and spirit. His scars must have been present to everyone. But in his father's presence, at least, the sordid past was never mentioned. The hurt and resentment did not soon disappear, but the father's correcting the elder brother indicates a determination to provide an environment where healing could take place. Gradually such a lad would resume his role as son, and if the family would hold its collective tongue, it would be for the father's sake. If the elder brother would forgive the prodigal, it would be for the sake of the father.

Similarly, if we would provide a healing environment, it too is for the sake of another, and this Other is Christ. Weatherhead presents this truth in yet another wonderful illustration:

"I am writing these words in a lovely garden under a cedar tree, on a perfect day in early summer. The air is sweet with the scent of cedar and of a lilac tree in full bloom. At my feet is a dog, Pete, aged and feeble..For some time his back was red-raw with disease, and his destruction contemplated..He is the property of Mike, the only son of

111

my host and hostess. Mike had to interrupt a university course to serve with the forces...Although now he (Pete) has fully recovered, he totters about the garden. He cannot run. He is not in any pain and appears to be happy..They saw the dog as something Mike loved. They would hardly like to meet Mike's eyes after the war if he said, 'Where's Pete?' and they could only answer that he had been 'put away' because he was a nuisance..and not worth having.''(50)

If we would refuse to be agents of healing and reconciliation for the love of Christ, then perhaps we ought to be such in the name of enlightened self-interest, if for no other reason. Even if we have no faith at all, we owe it to ourselves to be free from the effects of corrosive anger! And then there is the possibility of judgment! This portion of the Lord's Prayer reveals a reciprocity between forgiving and being forgiven. If memory persists after death, as illustrated in the story of the rich man and Lazarus where Abraham says, "Son...remember,"(51) surely this would prove the more intolerable the more we increase in spiritual insight. As we realize throughout eternity what our sin has cost a loving God, surely our sense of guilt will intensify!(52) As Maximos the Confessor writes: "He (the sinner) makes peace with all in order to be free from all the depravities of this present age when he departs to eternal life, and to receive from the Judge and Savior of the universe a just recompense for what he has done in this life."(53)

Again, we conclude with the words of St. Cyprian: "Having sought food for subsistence, we now seek remission of our sins, so that we who are fed by God may live in God and may provide not just for this present passing life but also for eternal life into which we can enter if our sins are forgiven."(54)

LEAD US NOT INTO TEMPTATION
BUT DELIVER US FROM EVIL

This petition of the Prayer we associate with those particular temptations that are so hard to resist in the midst of anxiety, desperation or despair. The Greek word *pierasmos,* which the prayer employs, may mean "to tempt" in this sense. This word, however, also conveys a deeper, stronger meaning — "to test." This is why most modern versions of the prayer employ variations of the phrase, "Do not put us to the test."

But why do we say, "Lead us not?" It would seem to imply that God willingly causes us to stumble, so we must plead that He not torment us so! While this idea is certainly an inaccurate view of the prayer's intent when taken by itself, it does nevertheless contain an element of truth. Evil is in the world, and because this is so, it must occur with the permission of God. St. Cyprian indicates this in his commentary when he says, "In this part of the prayer He shows us that the enemy is powerless against us without God's permission."(55)

Many students of the Lord's Prayer are convinced that Matthew's version is an "end time" prayer. Matthew may have believed that the time was at hand when God would judge the world, and that Christians must pray for the strength to endure this judgment, or Day of Wrath. Each time of testing, then, would be a preparation for that final great hour of trial, foretold by John's Apocalypse: "Because you have kept my commandments to endure trials, I will keep you safe in the time of trial which is going to come for the whole world." (Rev. 3:10-12)

Thus the prayer would seem to ask for fidelity in that decisive hour, and for every time of testing that would precede it. It is with this background that we must interpret these words of Paul to the Corinthian congregation: "The trials that you have had to bear are no more than people normally have. You can trust God not to let you be tried beyond your strength, and with any trial he will give you a way out of it and the strength to bear it." (I Cor. 10:11-13)

Evil is a fact of life in the world. The faith-response to evil is to believe that God places people in situations of trial where they may fail, and in situations which may be disastrous. The purpose, however, is not disaster, but triumph.(56) This is certainly the view expressed by scripture, whether in the Old Testament or the New. Job says, "Let him test me in the crucible: I shall come out pure gold." (23:10) The Epistle of James has this to say:

"My brothers, you will always have your trials but, when they come, try to treat them as a happy privilege; you understand that your faith is not only put to the test to make you patient, but patience too is to have its practical results so that you will become fully developed, complete, with nothing missing." (1:2-4)

First Peter adds: "This is a cause of great joy for you, even though you may for a short time have to bear being plagued by all sorts of trials; so that, when Jesus Christ is revealed, your faith will have been tested and proved like gold—only it is more precious than gold, which is corruptible even though it bears testing by fire—and then you will have praise and glory and honor." (1:6-7)

As we more or less regularly find ourselves "in temptation," Leonard Foley concludes that God must lead us there, "like the father putting his baby into the swimming pool and (more or less) letting him fend for himself."(57) As we have the promise that He will not try us beyond our strength, and that He will show us the way out of trial and give us the strength to bear it, this portion of the Prayer reminds us that He protects us even in the midst of trials that seem too hard to bear, and that in faith these trials may be turned to our good. We may emerge with a greater respect for our own limitations, a deeper consciousness of the power of evil, and a surer confidence in the power of God.

If we recognize, in the midst of the critical situation, that the "now" can become a movement toward the Kingdom, then the usual alternatives — acquiescence, despair or flight — are no longer appropriate. In faith, the situation becomes a test of faith which prepares us for the Kingdom. Whether we believe that our daily trials prepare us for some eschatological Day of Wrath, or our own personal crisis at the end of our earthly life, the same imperative applies: "I myself am not finally saved. And if I go to eternity having rejected the friendship of the Father, it will be a horrendous day for me, even if the world is not drowning in fire and millions of people are not screaming in agony. Can we still dare to think of a possible 'dies irae' for our single selves?"(58)

Between the times, the Exodus remains an appropriate figure for the test in our life of faith, as Metropolitan Anthony suggests:

"Look at the Exodus, at the Jews' awareness that they are not simply slaves but the people of God that had to become enslaved because of their moral weakness. They had to take risks because no one is ever freed by a slave owner, and they had to cross the Red Sea, but beyond the Red Sea it was not yet the promised land; it was a burning desert and they were aware of it and knew that they would have to cross it in the midst of great difficulties. And so are we when we decide to make a move that will liberate us from our enslavement: we must be aware that we shall be attacked by violence, by beguilement, by the same inner enemies that are our old habits, our old craving for security, and that nothing is promised us, except the desert beyond, and that we must accept the risks of the journey."(59)

Our journey proceeds as we refuse to give in to the seemingly hopeless situation, as we refuse to abandon our vision of God, and as we leap into the void in the confidence that God will protect us. To journey in faith means continual testing. Indeed, without the test there can be no movement, no growth in the Spirit, no visible presence of God in the world through us, and no Kingdom, either in us or for us! There will remain nothing for us but the "realism, dignity, and austerity of Hell."(60)

The second part of the petition asks the Father to deliver us from evil. The first part is a humble admission of need, while the second part, St. Cyprian observes, "covers everything harmful which the enemy tries against us in this world, but from which we can find sure and powerful protection if God delivers us and grants us His help, as we implore. When we say, 'Deliver us from evil,' there remains nothing further to ask for."(61)

The Greek word Matthew employs for evil bears two interpretations. I can refer to evil in a general sense, or refer specifically to the Evil One. Early in the life of the church, the West opted for the former interpretation, and the East, the latter. I believe that "the Evil One" more accurately represents the teachings of Jesus, who speaks about him many times. In Matthew 13:19, it is the Evil One who steals the good seed strewn along the path. In Matthew 5:37 Jesus says, "Say yes when you mean yes and no when you mean no. Anything beyond this is from the Evil One."

Twenty years ago, Flip Wilson, in his comedy routines, tried to make the devil cute. His "the devil made me do it," struck a whole generation as funny. C.S. Lewis referred to the "funny devil" routine in the Screwtape Letters. In this volume a junior devil is advised by his uncle that it is to Hell's advantage to make the patient (the young devil's human charge) think that spirits do not exist:

"I do not think you will have much difficulty in keeping the patient in the dark. The fact that 'devils' are predominantly comic figures in the modern imagination will help you. If any faint suspicion of your existence begins to arise in his mind, suggest to him a picture of something in red tights, and since he cannot believe in that...he therefore cannot believe in you."(62)

According to Jesus, the devils form a kingdom which is opposed to God's Kingdom. Paul tells the Ephesians that it is not human enemies against whom the faithful must struggle, but the Sovereignties

115

and Powers who originate the darkness in the world, the spiritual army of evil in the heavens. (6:12) He tells the Galatians, "..before we came of age we were as good as slaves to the elemental spirits of this world." (4:3) These are more than personal forces of evil. If they were merely personal, they would not be so destructive. Personal forces beget societal forces, and these wreak havoc in individuals and institutions In time, the whole of Creation is affected. "Man," Tillich suggests, "is split within himself. Life moves against itself through aggression, hate and despair."(63) And yet, Paul tells the Romans, there is hope. Creation still clings to the hope of being freed. (Rom. 8:20) The powers that originate the darkness of this world are overcome by the cross and the Resurrection, although their ultimate impotence has not as yet been made plain.

One of the tasks of the Christian, St. Maximos suggests, is to make it plain. It is not enough to simply pray this petition. We must bring it to fulfillment in our actions:

"Bringing the prayer to fulfillment through our actions, we shall manifestly proclaim God as our true Father by grace. We shall show that the Evil One, who is always tyrannically attempting to gain control of our nature through the shameful passions, is not the father of our life, and that we are not unwittingly exchanging life for death. For both God and the devil naturally impart their qualities to those who approach either of them: God bestows eternal life on those who love Him, while the devil, operating through temptations that are subject to our volition, causes the death of his followers."(64)

Pope John Paul II, in a recent statement, contrasts the Communion of Saints with what he calls "the communion of sin." Because of the presence of Christ in the world, made present by the Communion of Saints, we are enabled to rise above ourselves and to raise the world in the process. Within the communion of sin, however, "a soul that lowers itself through sin drags down with itself the Church and, in some way, the whole world."(65) He says further:

"Clearly sin is the product of man's freedom. But deep within its human reality there are factors at work which place it beyond the merely human, in the border area where man's conscience, will and sensitivity are in combat with the dark forces of evil which, according to St. Paul, are active in the world almost to the point of ruling it."(66)

If we are sensitive, we ought to be able to hear the audible groans of Creation. We know that most of the earth's resources are in the hands of the few, and consumed by a mere fraction of the earth's population. We should not require a Nathan to condemn us, saying, "You are the one!" We know—or ought to know—that our appetite for this world's goods is so insatiable that we have actually run out of places to hide our garbage.

The eco-system of the planet is under attack by hostile forces. We—the very creatures assigned dominion over it—are these forces. Our indiscriminate burning of fossil fuels, decades of chemical dumping, and the catastrophic results of our wars, may have already produced irreversible effects. Even if we discover the tools to reverse these effects in the next several decades, the quality of our earth and air has been diminished for generations to come. The enemy—as it were—is even now at the gates! Do we need a prophet to tell us who that enemy is?

We have been blind to other things as well. For years we believed—perhaps with some justification—that International Communism was out to destroy our way of life. But all the while we were building bombs another enemy was taking possession of our streets, our school yards, and perhaps the mind of a whole generation. At first we called this phenomenon the drug culture. Now the word "drug" almost seems a superfluous adjective, for "drugs" are now part and parcel of the whole.

If some were slow to address the problem of AIDS, it may have been because not a few believed it to be a judgment of God. Perhaps they were right, but in a much wider sense than they could have imagined. Now, what was once thought to be judgment for the few who "deserved" it, has become an epidemic for the many. Now the many are the heirs of a "judgment" once thought by some appropriate for the few!

What of the efficient slaughter of millions of the unborn, under the banner of "Pro-Choice" to which many of us are mute witnesses? In a bizarre way, the "Pro-Choice" slogan rings true. God respects our freedom so much that He gives us the power to choose life or death. By simple acquiescence we consent to a slaughter of the innocents on a scale that even Herod could not have comprehended. These generations will surely rise up and condemn us! The earth is not yet God's good world. Creation itself must be "snatched" from the Evil One!

St. Maximos, who reveals a magnificent grasp or our wretched estate, would show us the way out of it:

117

"For Christ, who has overcome the world (Jn. 16:33) is our leader. He arms us with the laws of the commandments, and by enabling us to reject the passions, He unites us in pure love with nature itself. Being the bread of life, of wisdom, spiritual knowledge, and righteousness, He arouses in us an insatiable desire for Himself. If we fulfill His Father's will He makes us co-worshippers with the angels, when in our conduct we imitate them as we should and so conform to the heavenly state."(67)

THINE IS THE KINGDOM

Matthew's version of the Lord's Prayer concludes with the doxology: "For thine is the kingdom and the power and the glory forever. Amen." A doxology like this comes from the worship of the synagogue, and may have been attached to the Prayer as an expression of devotion to the Prayer itself. If this is so, it must have happened late, because it does not appear in those manuscripts of the Gospel considered most reliable. Neither does it appear in Luke's version.

Although the doxology does appear in the King James Version of Matthew's prayer, the Revised Standard Version relegates it to a footnote, and virtually every other modern translation has followed its lead. The doxology has never appeared in any Roman Catholic version of the Bible, and is omitted in virtually every other modern, ecumenical version of the prayer. This might be called the case of the "disappearing doxology."

And yet these words, even if they are probably not the actual words of Jesus, are entirely appropriate. They confirm everything that the prayer would teach us: every good thing comes from God, belongs to Him and is sustained by Him. Metropolitan Anthony echoes the spirit of this doxology, and the Prayer itself, when he says that "the moment when we discover God within the situation, and that all things are God's and everything is of God (The Kingdom, Power and Glory, etc.) then we begin to enter this divine kingdom and acquire freedom."(68)

The Kingdom, which Jesus describes in numerous parables, is God's rule, or reign in the world. It is the pearl of great price. It is the dragnet that hauls forth all kinds of fish. It is a vineyard, and the wedding banquet of a king.

Matthew indicates that the Kingdom is no mere metaphor. One may enter it and there are even keys to it.(69) By the time of the writing of Matthew's Gospel, the Kingdom and the church had come to be regarded as intersecting, even though the church and the Kingdom were not believed to be necessarily synonymous. Although it is in Matthew's Gospel that we read the word "church" for the first time (16:18), we also find in this Gospel the parable of the weeds and the wheat. This leads Raymond Brown to conclude that Matthew's identification of the church with the Kingdom, and vice versa, is not complete.(70) In the parable, the children of the Kingdom are the good seed, while the children of the Evil One are the weeds. The weeds and the wheat are permitted to grow together until the harvest, lest a thorough weeding inadvertently pull out some of the good grain. When the Kingdom is fully come, "The Son of Man will summon His angels to gather out of the Kingdom all that do evil and throw them into a blazing furnace where there will be weeping and gnashing of teeth. Then the virtuous will shine with radiance like the sun in the Kingdom of their Father." (Matt. 13:41-43) (71)

In the meantime, the Kingdom may be found wherever Jesus's teachings are lived-out. In the meantime, the Kingdom is "a unique society where the voice of Jesus has not been stifled and remains normative."(72) Jesus answers the question about who is greatest in this Kingdom by the example of a little child. Brown continues:

"This is not because, as Romantics would have us think, the little child is thought of as lovable, or cuddly, or innocent, but because the child is helpless and dependent, with no power. In the Kingdom of Heaven God has supreme power and authority; closeness to God and therefore greatness in the kingdom comes according to the degree in which people surrender themselves to God, putting him first in their lives. When God rules in a person's life, then that person is great in God's Kingdom."(73)

The Kingdom stands in contrast to the world because the world operates with what Brown calls "the Caiaphas Principle."(74) Caiaphas was the High Priest who decreed Jesus's execution on the grounds that it would be better for one man to die for the nation than for the whole nation to be destroyed. (John 11:49-50) In the Kingdom, expediency is never an option. If one sheep is lost, stolen or strayed, the shepherd leaves the ninety-nine to look for it. In the world, and all too often in the church, expediency would dictate that the needs of the majority supersede the needs of the individual. To leave ninety-nine sheep in jeopardy to search for one that is lost seems impractical, short-sighted and downright foolish. There is, however, nothing calculating about the Kingdom.

In the Kingdom, one turns over the cloak as well as the coat to one who demands it. (Matt. 5:39-40) In the Kingdom, one sells all he or she has to follow Jesus (Matt. 19:21) and pays the worker who shows up at the end of the day the same wage as one who has toiled all day in the blazing sun. Although Brown observes that no institution can long survive in a world that is governed according to these principles, they "exemplify God's attitudes; and when they are put into practice, at that moment and in that place the Kingdom has been made a reality."(75) The coming of the Kingdom, and the set principles that we affirm when we pray "Thine is the Kingdom," would bring the end of life as we know it. (Matt. 24:14)

In the Kingdom, Power is given a new definition. It is a power the world cannot recognize, yet it is a power that always seems to have the last word. This power is exemplified by Christ's answer to Paul's plea that his thorn in the flesh be removed: "...my grace is enough for you: my power is at its best in weakness." (2 Cor. 12:9)

Each of Jesus's wilderness temptations has to do with power. In the end, He rejected as an illusion any power built upon selfish force and the selfish fear which is pride. Truly, that which the world calls power is the instrument of the Devil. If the Kingdom is the good leaven, power is the evil leaven. As the Kingdom goes about the redemption of the world silently and imperceptibly, what the world calls power goes about its corrupting work. Whether inconspicuously or with much sound and fury, its results are the same.

The gift of discernment which comes to the believer as a sign of rebirth, first becomes palpable within the sound and fury of the desert of temptation. Here one experiences the agony of the stripping away of the false selves, and the ecstasy that comes with the emergence of the deepest self, the God-directed self. St. Anthony expresses the struggle in this way: "(One)..who sits in solitude and is quiet has escaped from three wars: hearing, speaking, seeing: yet against one thing shall he continually battle: that is, his own heart."(76) But the storm does abate, and as it does, the gift appears.

The Second Book of Kings tells of the prophet Elijah's seeking the voice of God in the power of the wind, in the earthquake and the fire. Yet, in the midst of all this power, he heard only sound and fury. Finally, when he heard the voice of God, it was in the sound of a gentle breeze. Finally, we must put aside all the illusions of power proffered by the world. Then and only then shall we hear the still, small voice of God.

With the emergence of the deepest self, our eyes are opened to the power of the Spirit over the powers of the world. This awakening is beautifully described in one of our hymns:

"Age after age their tragic empires rise,
Built while they dream and in that dreaming weep:
Would man but wake from out his haunted sleep,
Earth might be fair and all men glad and wise."(77)

Glory is also given a new meaning in the Kingdom. A familiar symbol to most of us is the cross and crown. I remember from my childhood that this emblem was stitched to the pulpit scarf in our country church. When I asked my grandmother what it meant, she replied, "You can't have one without the other!" I don't suppose one ever fully understands what this means, as I certainly did not understand it then. The truth is, suffering is more or less what believers must expect. The mysterious companion on the road to Emmaus asks, "Was it not ordained that Christ should suffer and so enter into his glory?" (Luke 24:26) If this is the model that Christ lived-out, it ought not surprise us when we are called to live it out as well. Yet, as Geoffery Wainwright assures us: "Apparent God-forsakenness, of which suffering is the sharpest sign, may in fact be a moment of growth in communion with a God who is never really absent from a creation which he never ceases to love."(78)

Faith, as suggested earlier, transforms "breakdown" into "breakthrough." It is through suffering for Him and for His name that we reflect His glory.

When James and John asked for glory in the Kingdom, it was glory for its own sake. Jesus's response that they did not know for what they were asking, could easily be directed to us. Glory for its own sake is what Andy Warhol talked about when he remarked that in America everybody will be famous for fifteen minutes. The pursuit of glory for its own sake is sowing the wind and reaping the whirlwind. (Hos. 8:7)

Glory in the Kingdom comes of obedience to God. Through obedience, as Paul says, we, with our faces reflecting like mirrors the brightness of our Lord, become brighter and brighter as we are transformed into the image that we reflect. (2 Cor. 4:6)

In the world, as Grey's Elegy puts it, "the paths of glory lead but to the grave." In the Kingdom, it is through the grave that we shall receive glory, when at last we shall appear with Him in Glory. (Col. 3:4) In the Kingdom, those who are closest to Christ most resemble Him in glory, and when we see them, we behold not them but Christ Himself.

Years ago, when I was a student pastor, one of my parishioners, an elderly lady named Nora, was slowly dying of a disease for which there was as yet no name. She was a simple country woman and her children described her as "peculiar." While hospitalization would certainly have prolonged her life, she insisted that she was going to "wait for Jesus" in the same bedroom where she had birthed her children and where she had kept vigil the night her husband died. During our last visit, I noticed that the room had a peculiar odor, but one not usually associated with sickrooms. For some time I couldn't identify it, but suddenly it came to me. "Nora," I asked, "did you have some papering done in here?" She smiled and replied softly, "Now, it wouldn't do to have Jesus come and have to look at old wallpaper!" "No," I replied, "I suppose not!" I sat there thinking that there would have been something flatly incredible about that interchange were it not for the fact that her face shone like that of an angel. She never had much in the way of glory, but the glory she reflected that day was palpable—at least as real as the smell of freshly-applied wallpaper.

A doxology is a form of praise. In the doxology that ends the Lord's Prayer, we surrender the Kingdom, the Power and the Glory to God. As Nora demonstrated to all who knew her, surrender is the truest praise. It is also the only way to the Kingdom, the Power and the Glory.

(1) Bloom, Anthony, *Living Prayer,* Templegate Publishers, Springfield IL, 1966, p. 20.

(2) Foley, Leonard O.F.M., *Slowing Down The Our Father,* St. Anthony Messenger Press, 1986, p. 98.

(3) Mottola, Anthony (Trans.), *The Spiritual Exercises of St. Ignatius,* Image/Doubleday, a division of Bantam Doubleday Dell Publishing Group, Inc., 666 Fifth Avenue, New York, NY 10103, 1964, p. 107.

(4) Thielicke, Helmut, *Being a Christian When The Chips Are Down,* Anderson, George H. (Trans.), Fortress Press., Phila., p. 52.

(5) *Op. Cit.,* Bloom, pps. 43-4.

(6) Killinger, John, *The God Named Hallowed: The Lord's Prayer For Today*, Abingdon Press, Nashville, 1988, p. 17.

(7) *Ibid.*, p. 17.

(8) Leech, Kenneth, *True Prayer: An Invitation to Christian Spirituality*, Harper & Row Publishers, San Francisco, 1980, p. 22.

(9) Bonin, Edmond (Trans.), *The Lord's Prayer By St. Cyprian of Carthage*, Christian Classics, PO Box 30, Westminster, MD 21157, 1983, p. 33.

(10) *Ibid.*, p. 35.

(11) *Ibid.*, p. 35.

(12) Luibheid, Colm and Russell, Norman (Trans.), *John Climacus: The Ladder of Divine Ascent*, Paulist Press, New York, 1982, p. 236.

(13) *Op. Cit.*, Leech, pps. 49-50.

(14) *Ibid.*, p. 62.

(15) *Op. Cit.*, Killinger, p. 26.

(16) *Op. Cit.*, Leech, p. 34.

(17) Lewis, C.S., *The Problem of Pain*, Macmillan Paperbacks Edition, 1962, The Macmillan Company, New York, p. 52.

(18) *Op. Cit.*, Leech, p. 135.

(19) *Op. Cit.*, Bonin, p. 35.

(20) *Ibid.*, pps. 38-39.

(21) *The Methodist Hymnal*, The United Methodist Publishing House, Nashville, 1964, #138.

(22) *Op. Cit.*, Bloom, pps. 38-39.

(23) *Op. Cit.*, Leech, p. 79.

(24) *Op. Cit.*, Bloom, p. 38.

(25) *Op. Cit.*, Leech, p. 69.

(26) Merton, Thomas, *The Ascent to Truth*, A Harvest/HBJ Book, Harcourt Brace Jovanovich, Publishers, San Diego, New York and London, 1979, p. 282.

(27) *Op. Cit.*, Foley, p. 40.

(28) *Ibid.*, Foley, p. 59.

(29) *Op. Cit.*, Bonin, p. 53.

(30) *Op. Cit.*, Leech, p. 111.

(31) *Ibid.*, p. 115.

(32) Palmer, G.E.H., Sherrard, Philip, and Ware, Kallistos (Trans.), *The Philokalia, Vol. 2.*, compiled by St. Nicodemus of the Holy Mountain and St. Macarios of Corinth, Faber and Faber, London and Boston, 1986, pps. 299-300.

(33) *Ibid.*, p. 299.

(34) *Op. Cit.*, Bloom, p. 33.

(35) *Op. Cit.*, Leech, p. 94.

(36) *Ibid.*, p. 110.

(37) *Ibid.*, p. 110.

(38) *Op. Cit.*, Bonin, pps. 55-56.

(39) Tillich, Paul, *The Shaking of the Foundations*, Charles Scribner's Sons, New York, 1948, p. 155.

(40) *Ibid.*, pps. 154-155.

(41) *Op. Cit.*, Leech, p. 130.

(42) *Op. Cit.*, Bloom, p. 31.

(43) *Op. Cit.*, Tillich, p. 161.

(44) *Op. Cit.*, Bloom, p. 30.

(45) *Op. Cit.*, Tillich, p. 162.

(46) *Op. Cit.*, Bloom, p. 31.

(47) Weatherhead, Leslie D., *The Meaning of the Cross*, A Festival Book, 1982, Abingdon Press, Nashville, p. 144.

(48) *Ibid.*, p. 144.

(49) *Ibid.*, p. 144.

(50) *Ibid.*, pps. 147-148.

(51) *Ibid.*, p. 142.

(52) *Ibid.*, p. 142.

(53) *Op. Cit.*, *The Philokalia*, p. 302.

(54) *Op. Cit.*, Bonin, p. 66.

(55) *Ibid.*, p. 75.

(56) *Op. Cit.*, Leech, pps. 145-146.

(57) *Op. Cit.*, Foley, p. 84.

(58) *Ibid.*, p. 88.

(59) *Op. Cit.*, Bloom, pps. 29-30.

(60) Lewis, C.S., *The Screwtape Letters*, Collins/Fontana Books., London and Glasgow., 1963., p. 58.

(61) *Op. Cit.*, Bonin, p. 80.

(62) *Op. Cit.*, Lewis, p. 40.

(63) *Op. Cit.*, Tillich, p. 158.

(64) *Op. Cit.*, *The Philokalia*, p. 304.

(65) Pope John Paul II, *Apostolic Exhortation of Reconciliation and Penance*, as cited by Foley, p. 92.

(66) *Ibid.*, p. 92.

(67) *Op. Cit.*, *The Philokalia*, pps. 303-304.

(68) *Op. Cit.*, Bloom, p. 25.

(69) Brown, Raymond E., *The Churches The Apostles Left Behind*, Paulist Press, New York/Ramsey, 1984, p. 51.

(70) *Ibid.*, pps. 51-52.

(71) *Ibid.*, p. 52.

(72) *Ibid.*, p. 138.

(73) *Ibid.*, p. 140.

(74) *Ibid.*, p. 141.

(75) *Ibid.*, p. 142.

(76) *Op. Cit.*, Leech, pps. 178-179.

(77) *The Book of Hymns*, The United Methodist Publishing House, Nashville, 1964, #475.

(78) Wainright, Geoffery, *Doxology: A Systematic Theology*, Oxford University Press, New York, 1980, p. 43.

THE CANONICAL HOURS

We are creatures of time, and God reveals Himself to His children in time. Paul says to the Galatians, "...when the appointed time came, God sent his Son.(4:4)." He reveals Himself in the rhythm of life: as light turns to darkness and to the light again; as sleep gives ways to waking, and waking to work; and as work returns to reflection and rest again.

There is chronological time, when, as the poet says, "time turns round itself in an obedient circle."(1) This is mechanical time, time-table time, time where the light of the Presence is not perceived:

"The heavens declare the glory of God,
the vault of heaven proclaims his handiwork;
day discourses to day,
night to night hands on the knowledge.
No utterance at all, no speech,
no sound that anyone can hear;
yet their voice goes out through all the earth,
and their message to the ends of the world." (Ps. 19:1-14)

There is kairotic time, or sacred time. In truth, as time is part of God's good Creation, time is never "chronos," but always "kairos." Faithful men and women from the time of the church's beginnings have perceived this. Their communities labored to "redeem the time," to place an overlay of intentionality upon time. It is within this overlay that the Created perceives its oneness with its Creator.

Part of their legacy is the Christian Year, which stretches from Advent through Epiphany, from Ash Wednesday through Good Friday, and from Easter through Pentecost. Another part of that legacy which is largely unknown is the Canonical Hours. Within this structure is found "the peaceful alternation of work and rest," alongside the challenge to "stay awake and pray with Christ in Gethsemane."(2)

127

By the Third Century, the structure of the Canonical Hours, whether derived from the hours of prayer in the synagogues, or the Roman division of the day into four "hours" — Prima (first); Tertia (third); Sexta (sixth) and Nona (ninth) — had been established. By the time of Benedict and his Rule (AD 543), the four watches of the night were included as an integral part of this structure. The first watch of the evening had become Vespers (Lat. vespera: evenings). The second, at midnight, had become Compline (Lat. completa: complete). The third, at cockcrow, had become Matins (Lat. Matuta: the goddess of the morning), and the fourth, at dawn, had become Lauds (Lat. laudare: "to praise or extol").

From the beginning the Canonical Hours have been corporate by nature. It is "people prayer." Prayer as the whole community, and prayer as a microcosm of the universal church. As the Introduction to Common Prayer at Taizé puts it, "Common prayer is a different exercise from the more-or-less silent waiting on God in our rooms with the door shut, which we are inclined to consider as the main form of praying."(3)

In his Rule, Benedict identified unceasing praise of God as the chief purpose of the church. If this is true, then the Canonical Hours, as Evelyn Underhill puts it, are "the ordained form within which the whole church performs from hour to hour, by night and day, that unceasing praise."(4)

Yet, the Canonical Hours have another function as well. Brother Roger of Taizé tells us that perseverance is the way to focus our attention upon Christ through the dull days of our life.(5) In other words, we must knock upon the door until it is opened. For sometimes, "the light of the presence can...flash through our prayer and there are no words to describe that experience."(6)

In the exercise that follows I have divided a twenty-four hour day into eight three-hour segments which correspond to the historic Canonical Hours. This structure is intended for corporate worship and is specifically designed for a retreat setting where two or three are gathered in Christ's name. Not everyone has the opportunity to spend time in a monastic community where the Hours are observed. This exercise may provide a helpful alternative.

The Hours in this exercise lift-up eight "Holy Mysteries" which respectively correspond to each three-hour segment. They are: first, the absence of God experienced by the disciples in those dreadful hours after the crucifixion; second, the Resurrection; third, Pentecost; fourth, Epiphany; fifth, the Baptism of our Lord; sixth, the Transfiguration; seventh the Eucharist; eighth, Gethsemane. The eighth hour ends in total darkness, which begins the cycle all over again.

To follow the Hours through one complete cycle is to begin to perceive the sacred nature of time itself. This truth enables us to see our own life, and our life together, as part of God's great plan revealed in time.

This version of the Hours, while it attempts to be faithful to the structure of the historical models, provides a time for free prayer in each liturgy. This stresses the corporate nature of the exercise and reduces the prospect that the structure might become yet another rigid mechanism. The written code kills, but the Spirit brings life.

VESPERS
Theme: Eucharist — Time: 6:00 - 9:00 PM.

INVITATORY:

Liturgist: Let us implore our Redeemer, who suffered his passion, was buried and rose again from the dead, saying:

O Christ, we adore you.

Community: O Christ, we adore you.

L: Lord our master, for us you became obedient unto death, teach us to do your Father's will.

C: O Christ, we adore you.

L: Lord our Life, by dying on the Cross you have conquered death and the powers of darkness, enable us to share in your death and in your resurrection into glory.

C: O Christ, we adore you.

L: Lord our Strength, you were despised by men, humiliated as a condemned criminal, teach us true humility.

C: O Christ, we adore you.

L: Lord our Salvation, you gave your life for love of your brothers and sisters, teach us to love one another with that same love.

C: O Christ, we adore you.

L: Lord our God, with hands outstretched on the Cross, you draw all to yourself, gather into your Kingdom the scattered children of God.

C: O Christ, we adore you. Amen. (7)

HYMN:

Let all mortal flesh keep silence
And with fear and trembling stand;
Ponder nothing earthly minded,
For with blessing in his hand,
Christ our God to earth
Descendeth,
Our full homage to demand.
King of kings, yet born of Mary
As of old on earth he stood,
Lord of Lords, in human vesture
In the body and the blood
He will give to all
The Faithful
His own self for heavenly food.
Rank on rank the host of heaven
Spreads its vanguard on the way,
As the Light of light descendeth
From the realms of endless day,
That the powers of hell
May vanish
As the darkness clears away.
At his feet the six-winged seraph
Cherubim with sleepless eye,
Veil their faces to the presence,
As with ceaseless voice they cry
Alleluia
Alleluia
Alleluia, Lord most high!(8)

Liturgist: Make a joyful noise unto God, all ye lands.
Community: Let Psalms declare the glory of his name.

PSALM:

Community Right: Alleluia!
Praise Yahweh, my soul!
Community Left: I mean to praise Yahweh all my life,
I mean to sing to my God as long as I live.
R: Do not put your trust in men of power,

or in any mortal man—he cannot save,
L: he yields his breath and goes back to the earth he came from,
and on that day all his schemes perish.
R: Happy the man who has the God of Jacob to help him,
whose hope is fixed on Yahweh his God,
L: maker of heaven and earth,
and the sea, and all that these hold.
R: Yahweh, forever faithful
gives justice to those denied it,
gives food to the hungry,
gives liberty to prisoners.
L: Yahweh restores sight to the blind,
R: Yahweh straightens the bent,
L: Yahweh protects the stranger,
R: he keeps the orphan and widow.
L: Yahweh loves the virtuous,
R: and frustrates the wicked.
L: Yahweh reigns forever,
your God, Zion from age to age. (Psalm 146)

Liturgist: O Lord, I will meditate on your precepts.
Community: I will delight in your statutes; I will not forget your word.

OLD TESTAMENT LESSON: (Exodus 24:3-11)

Liturgist: Your teachings are wonderful; I obey them with all my heart.
Community: The explanation of your teachings gives light, and wisdom to the inexperienced.

NEW TESTAMENT LESSON: (Mark 14:17-31)
SILENCE
FREE PRAYER
APPOINTED PRAYER: (All)
    Almighty Father, whose dear Son, on the night before he suffered, instituted the Sacrament of His Body and Blood, mercifully grant that we may receive it thankfully in remembrance of Jesus Christ our Lord, who in these holy mysteries gives us a pledge of eternal life; and who

now lives and reigns with you and the Holy Spirit, one God, forever and ever. Amen.(9)

(Here may follow a brief service of Holy Communion)

Liturgist: I thank you, Lord, with all my heart; I sing praise to you.

Community: You answered me when I called to you; with your strength you strengthened me.

L: You will do everything you have promised me;

C: Lord, your love is constant forever. Complete the work that you have begun. Amen.

COMPLINE
Theme: Gethsemane — Time: 9:00-12:00 Midnight
INVITATORY:

Liturgist: O my people, what have I done to you? How have I grieved you? Answer Me!

Community: Lord, have mercy!

L: I freed you from slavery, I engulfed your enemy: you handed me over, you jeered at me. O my people, what have I done to you? How have I grieved you? Answer me!

C: Christ, have mercy!

L: I opened the sea before you: you opened my side with your spear! O my people, what have I done to you? How have I grieved you? Answer me!

C: Lord, have mercy!

L: I moved before you in the pillar of cloud: you led me to Pilate! O my people, what have I done to you? How have I grieved you? Answer me!

C: Christ, have mercy!

L: I watched over you in the desert and fed you with manna: you struck me and scourged me! O my people, what have I done to you? How have I grieved you? Answer me!

C: Lord, have mercy!

L: I gave you from the rock living waters of salvation: You gave me gall to drink, you quenched my thirst with vinegar! O my people, what have I done to you? How have I grieved you? Answer me!

C: Christ, have mercy!

L: I struck down kings for you: you struck me with a reed! O my people, what have I done to you? How have I grieved you? Answer me!

C: Lord, have mercy!

L: I put the sceptre into your hand, I made you a royal people: you crowned me with the crown of thorns! O my people, what have I done to you? How have I grieved you? Answer me!

C: Christ, have mercy!

L: I made you great by my boundless power: you hanged me on the gallows of a cross. O my people, what have I done to you? How have I grieved you? Answer me!

C: God, holy; God, strong and holy;

God, holy and immortal: have pity on us. Amen.(10)

HYMN:

'Tis midnight, and on olive's brow
The star is dimmed that lately shone:
'Tis midnight in the garden now
The suffering Savior prays alone.
'Tis midnight, and from all removed
The Savior wrestles lone with fears;
E'en that disciple whom he loved
Heeds not his master's grief and tears.
'Tis midnight, and from others' guilt
The Man of Sorrows weeps in blood;
Yet he that hath in anguish knelt
Is not forsaken by his God.
'Tis midnight, and from heavenly plains
Is borne the song that angels know
Unheard by mortals are the strains
That sweetly soothe the Savior's woe.(11)

Liturgist: Make a joyful noise unto God, all ye lands.
Community: Let Psalms declare the glory of his name.

PSALM:

Community Right: My God, my God, why have you deserted me?
How far from saving me, the words I groan!
Community Left: I call all day, my God, but you never answer,
all night long I call and cannot rest.
R: Yet, Holy One, you
who make your home in the praises of Israel,

L: in you our fathers put their trust,
they trusted and you rescued them;
R: They called to you for your help and they were saved,
they never trusted you in vain.
L: Yet here am I, now more worm than man,
scorn of mankind, jest of the people,
R: all who see me jeer at me,
they toss their heads and sneer,
L: "He relied on Yahweh, let Yahweh save him!
if Yahweh is his friend, let Him rescue him!"
R: Yet you drew me out of the womb,
you entrusted me to your mother's breasts;
L: placed on your lap from my birth,
from my mother's womb you have been my God.
R: Do not stand aside: trouble is near,
I have no one to help me!
L: A herd of bulls surrounds me,
strong bulls of Bashan close in on me;
R: Their jaws are agape for me,
like lions tearing and roaring.
L: I am like water draining away,
my bones are all disjointed,
my heart is like wax,
melting inside me;
R: my palate is drier than a potsherd
and my tongue is stuck to my jaw.
L: A pack of dogs surrounds me,
a gang of villains closes me in;
R: They tie my hand and foot
and leave me lying in the dust of death.
L: I can count every one of my bones,
and there they glare at me, gloating;
R: they divide my garments among them
and cast lots for my clothes.
L: Do not stand aside, Yahweh.
O my strength, come quickly to my help;
R: rescue my soul from the sword,
my dear life from the paw of the dog,
L: Save me from the lion's mouth,

134

my poor soul from the wild bull's horns!
R: Then I shall proclaim your name to my brothers,
praise you in the full assembly:
L: you who fear Yahweh, praise him!
Entire race of Jacob, glorify him!
Entire race of Israel, revere him!
R: For he has not despised
or disdained the poor man in his poverty,
has not hidden his face from him,
but has answered him when he called. (Psalm 22:1-24)

Liturgist: O Lord, I will meditate on your precepts.
Community: I will delight in your statutes; I will not forget your word.

OLD TESTAMENT LESSON: (Isaiah 52:13-53:12)
Liturgist: In the night I think of you, Lord, and I obey your law.
Community: This is my happiness: I obey your commands.

NEW TESTAMENT LESSON: (John 18:19-40 [long])
                               (John 19:17-30 [short])
SILENCE
FREE PRAYER
APPOINTED PRAYER: (All)
     Almighty God, we pray you graciously to behold this your family,
for whom our Lord Jesus Christ was willing to be betrayed, and given
into the hands of sinners, and to suffer death upon the cross; who now
lives and reigns with you and Holy Spirit, one God, forever and ever.
Amen.(12)

Liturgist: I trust in you; in the morning remind me of your constant
love.
Community: My prayers go up to you; show me the way I should go.
Amen.

MATINS
Theme: The Absence of God — Time: 12 Midnight-3:00 AM
INVITATORY:
Liturgist: Let us implore our Redeemer who suffered his passion,
was buried and rose again from the dead, saying:

O Christ, we adore you.

Community: O Christ, we adore you.

L: O Savior Christ, your grief-stricken Mother was present at your cross and burial: enable us to share in your Passion at our times of testing.

C: O Christ, we adore you.

L: O Lord Christ, like a seed of wheat fallen to the ground, you have borne the fruit of the life of God: may we die to sin and live for God.

C: O Christ, we adore you.

L: O Christ, the new Adam, you descended into the kingdom of the dead to set the good free from captivity: may your voice be heard by all who have died to sin, that they may live.

C: O Christ, we adore you.

L: O Christ, Son of the living God, through baptism we have been buried with you in death: make us partners in your resurrection, that we may walk in newness of life.

C: O Christ, we adore you.(13)

HYMN:
Jesus, keep me near the cross;
There a precious fountain,
Free to all, a healing stream,
Flows from Calvary's mountain.
Near the cross, a trembling soul
Love and mercy found me;
There the bright and morning star
Shed its beams around me.
Near the cross! O Lamb of God,
Bring its scenes before me;
Help me walk from day to day
With its shadow o'er me.
Near the cross I'll watch and wait,
Hoping, trusting ever,
Till I reach the golden strand
Just beyond the river.
Refrain: In the cross, in the cross
Be my glory ever
Till my raptured soul shall find

Rest beyond the river.(14)

Liturgist: Make a joyful noise unto God, all ye lands.
Community: Let Psalms declare the glory of his name.

PSALM:
Community Right: Lord, you have been our refuge age after age.
Community Left: Before the mountains were born,
before the earth or the world came to birth,
you were God from all eternity and forever.
R: You can turn man back into dust
by saying, "Back to what you were, you sons of men!"
L: To you, a thousand years are a single day,
a yesterday now over, an hour of the night.
R: You brush men away like waking dreams,
they are like grass
L: sprouting and flowering in the morning,
withered and dry before dusk.
R: We too are burned up by your anger
and terrified by your fury;
L: having summoned up our sins
you inspect our secrets by your own light.
R: Our days dwindle under your wrath,
our lives are over in a breath
L: —our life lasts for seventy years,
eighty with good health,
but they all add up to anxiety and trouble—
over in a trice, and then they are gone.
R: Who yet has felt the full force of your fury,
or learned to fear the violence of your rage?
L: Teach us to count how few days we have
and so gain wisdom of heart.
R: Relent, Yahweh! How much longer do we have?
Take pity on your servants!
L: Let us wake in the morning filled with your love
and sing and be happy all our days;
R: make our future as happy as our past was sad,
those years when you were punishing us.
L: Let your servants see what you can do for them,

let their children see your glory.

R: May all the sweetness of the Lord be on us!
Make all we do succeed. (Psalm 90)

Liturgist: O Lord, I will meditate on your precepts.
Community: I will delight in your statutes; I will not forget your word.

OLD TESTAMENT LESSON: (Job 14:1-14)
Liturgist: I believe, I shall see the goodness of God in the land of living.
Community: Hope in God, take heart and be of good courage!

NEW TESTAMENT LESSON: (Matthew 27:57-66)
SILENCE
FREE PRAYER
APPOINTED PRAYER: (All)
    O God, Creator of heaven and earth: Grant that, as the crucified body of your dear Son was laid in the tomb and rested on that holy Sabbath, so we may await with him, and rise with him to newness of life; who now lives and reigns with you and the Holy Spirit, one God, forever and ever. Amen. (15)
Liturgist: Save us Lord, when we are awake;
Community: Guard us, Lord, when we are asleep;
L: Awake we will watch with Christ,
C: And asleep we will rest in peace.(16)

LAUDS
Theme: Resurrection — Time: 3:00-6:00 AM.
INVITATORY:
(The Paschal Candle is lit)
Liturgist: How holy is this night, when wickedness is put to flight, and sin washed away. It restores innocence to the fallen, and joy to those who mourn. It casts out pride and hatred, and brings peace and concord.
Community: How blessed is this night, when earth and heaven are joined and man is reconciled to God.(17)
L: Alleluia, Christ is risen, Alleluia!
C: He really is risen, Alleluia, Alleluia!
L: The stone has been rolled away, Alleluia!

C: —From the mouth of the tomb, Alleluia, Alleluia!
L: He is no longer dead, Alleluia!
C: The Living One is risen again, Alleluia! Alleluia!
L: He has conquered by the Cross, Alleluia! Alleluia!
C: He has come out of the tomb, Alleluia, Alleluia!
L: Alleluia, our hope is in him, Alleluia!
C: He will take us to glory, Alleluia, Alleluia!

HYMN:
Thou hidden source of calm repose
Thou all-sufficient love divine,
My help and refuge from my foes,
Secure I am if thou art mine;
And lo! From sin and grief and shame,
I hide me, Jesus, in thy name.
Thy mighty name salvation is,
And keeps my happy soul above;
Comfort it brings, and power and peace
And joy and everlasting love:
To me, with thy great name, are given
Pardon and holiness and heaven.
Jesus, my all-in-all thou art:
My rest in toil, my ease in pain,
The healing of my broken heart,
In war my peace, in loss my gain,
My smile beneath the tyrant's frown:
In shame my glory and my crown.
In want my plentiful supply,
In weakness my almighty power,
In bonds my perfect liberty,
My light in Satan's darkest hour,
In grief my joy unspeakable,
My life in death, my heaven in hell.(19)

Liturgist: Make a joyful noise unto God, all ye lands.
Community: Let Psalms declare the glory of his name.

PSALM:

Community Right: Alleluia! Give thanks to Yahweh, for he is good, his love is everlasting!

Community Left: Let the House of Israel say it, "His love is everlasting."

R: I was pressed, pressed, about to fall,
but Yahweh came to my help;

L: Yahweh is my strength and my song,
he has been my savior.

R: Shouts of joy and safety in the tents of the virtuous: Yahweh's right hand is wreaking havoc,

L: Yahweh's right hand is winning,
Yahweh's right hand is wreaking havoc!

R: No, I shall not die, I shall live
to recite the deeds of Yahweh;

L: Though Yahweh has punished me often,
he has not abandoned me to death.

R: Open the gates of virtue to me,
I will come in and give thanks to Yahweh.

L: This is Yahweh's gateway,
through which the virtuous may enter.

R: I thank you for having heard me,
you have been my Savior.

L: It was the stone rejected by the builders
that proved to be the keystone;

R: this is Yahweh's doing
and it is wonderful to see.

L: This is the day made memorable by Yahweh,
what immense joy for us!

R: Please, Yahweh, please save us.
Please, Yahweh, please give us prosperity.

L: Blessings on him who comes in the name of Yahweh!
We bless you from the house of Yahweh.

R: Yahweh is God, he smiles on us.
With branches in your hands draw up in
procession as far as the horns of the altar,

L: You are my God, I give you thanks,
I extol you, my God;
I give you thanks for having heard me,
You have been my Savior.

R: Give thanks to Yahweh, for he is good,
his love is everlasting! (Psalm 118:1-2;13-29)
Liturgist: O Lord, I will meditate on your precepts.
Community: I will delight in your statutes; I will not forget your word.

OLD TESTAMENT LESSON: (Exodus 15:1-11)
Liturgist: You sleeper, awake,
Community: Rise from the dead!
L: Upon you will shine the light
C: Jesus Christ, Alleluia!(20)
-Or-
Liturgist: You are God: we praise you;
Community: You are the Lord: we acclaim you;
L: You are the eternal Father:
C: All creation worships you.
L: To you all angels, all the powers of heaven,
C: Cherubim and Seraphim, sing in endless praise:
L: Holy, Holy, Holy Lord, God of power and might,
C: heaven and earth are full of your glory.
L: The glorious company of the apostles praise you.
C: The noble fellowship of the prophets praise you.
L: The white-robed army of martyrs praise you.
C: Throughout the world the holy Church acclaims you:
L: Father, of majesty unbounded,
C: your true and only Son, worthy of all worship,
L: and the Holy Spirit, advocate and guide.
C: You, Christ, are the king of glory,
L: The eternal Son of the Father.
C: When you became man to set us free,
L: You did not spurn the virgin's womb.
C: You overcame the sting of death,
L: And opened the kingdom of heaven to all believers.
C: You are seated on God's right hand in glory.
L: We believe that you will come, and be our judge.
C: Come then, Lord, and help your people,
L: bought with the price of your own blood
C: and bring us with your saints
L: to glory everlasting.
C: Save your people, Lord, and bless your inheritance.

L: Govern and uphold them now and always.
C: Day by day we bless you.
L: We praise your name forever.
C: Keep us today, Lord, from all sin.
L: Have mercy upon us, Lord, have mercy;
C: Lord, show us your love and mercy;
L: for we put our trust in you.
C: In you, Lord, is our hope:
L: and we shall never hope in vain.(21)

NEW TESTAMENT LESSON   (Luke 24:1-11)
SILENCE
FREE PRAYER
APPOINTED PRAYER: (All)
    O God, who made this most holy night to shine with the glory of
the Lord's resurrection: stir up in your Church that Spirit of adoption
which is given to us in Baptism, that we, being renewed both in body
and mind, may worship you in sincerity and truth; through Jesus Christ
our Lord, who lives and reigns with you, in the unity of the Holy Spirit,
one God, now and forever. Amen.

Liturgist: May the God of peace sanctify us wholly, keeping us
blameless in body, mind and soul for the coming of our Lord Jesus
Christ.
Community: Amen.

PRIME
Theme: Pentecost — Time: 6:00-9:00 AM.
INVITATORY:
Liturgist: Send forth your Spirit, Lord,
Community: Renew the face of the earth.
L: Creator Spirit, come,
C: Inflame our waiting hearts.
L: Your Spirit fills the world,
C: And knows our every word.
L: Glory to God our Father,
C: To Jesus Christ, the Son,
L: To you, O Holy Spirit,
C: Now and forevermore.

L: You are, you were, you come,
C: Eternal, living God!(22)
HYMN:
See how great a flame aspires
Kindled by a spark of grace!
Jesus' love the nations fires
Sets the kingdoms on a blaze.
To bring fire on earth he came;
Kindled in some hearts it is:
O that all might catch the flame,
All partake the glorious bliss!
When he first the work begun,
Small and feeble was his day.
Now the Word doth swiftly run;
Now it wins its widening way;
More and more it spreads and grows,
Ever mighty to prevail;
Sin's strongholds it now o'erthrows,
Shakes the trembling gates of hell.
Sons of God your Savior praise,
He the door hath opened wide;
He hath given the word of grace;
Jesus' word is glorified.
Jesus mighty to redeem,
He alone the work hath wrought;
Worthy is the work of him,
Him who spake a world from naught.
Saw ye not the cloud arise,
Little as a human hand?
Now it spreads along the skies,
Hangs o'er all the thirsty land;
Lo! the promise of a shower
Drops already from above;
But the Lord will shortly pour
All the spirit of his love.(23)

Liturgist: Make a joyful noise unto God, all ye lands.
Community: Let Psalms declare the glory of his name.

PSALM:

Community Right: Yahweh, what variety you have created,
arranging everything so wisely!
Earth is completely full of things you have made:
Community Left: among them the vast expanse of ocean,
teeming with countless creatures,
creatures large and small,
R: with the ships going to and fro
and Leviathan whom you made to amuse you.
L: All creatures depend on you
to feed them throughout the year;
R: you provide the food they eat,
with generous hand you satisfy their hunger.
L: You turn your face away, they suffer,
you stop their breath, they die
and revert to dust.
R: You give breath, fresh life begins,
you keep renewing the world.
L: Glory forever to Yahweh!
May Yahweh find joy in what he creates,
R: at whose glance the earth trembles,
at whose touch the mountains smoke!
L: I mean to sing to Yahweh all my life,
I mean to play for my God as long as I live.
R: May these reflections of mine give him pleasure,
L: May sinners vanish from the earth
and the wicked exist no more!
Bless Yahweh, my soul. (Psalm 104:24-35)

Liturgist: O Lord, I will meditate on your precepts.
Community: I will delight in your statutes; I will not forget your word.

OLD TESTAMENT LESSON: (Joel 2:28-29)
Liturgist: Come Holy Spirit, from heaven shine with your glorious
light!
Community: Most kindly, warming Light! Enter the inmost depth of
our hearts, for we are faithful to you. Without your presence, we have
nothing worthy, nothing pure.(24)

NEW TESTAMENT LESSON: (John 20:19-23)
SILENCE
FREE PRAYER
APPOINTED PRAYER: (All)

Almighty God, who opened the way of eternal life to every race
and nation by the promised gift of your Holy Spirit: shed abroad this
gift throughout the world by the preaching of the Gospel, that it may
reach to the ends of the earth; through Jesus Christ our Lord, who lives
and reigns with you, in the unity of the Holy Spirit, one God, forever
and ever. Amen.(25)

Liturgist: May the grace of our Lord Jesus Christ, the love of God
the Father and the Communion of the Holy Spirit, be with us all.
Community: Amen.

TERCE
Theme: Epiphany — Time: 9:00AM.-12 Noon

INVITATORY:
Liturgist: Return to the Lord, he has pity on you—
—to God, he is all forgiveness.
Community: Pity me, Lord, in your kindness,
L: In your love blot out my sin,
C: Wash me of all my faults.
L: Cleanse me from my misdeeds.
C: For I know my sin,
L: My fault is ever before me.
C: Against you, you only, have I sinned.
L: I have done evil in your sight.
C: To him who reigns from the throne, and to the Lamb
L: Praise and honor, glory and power forever and ever.(26)
HYMN:
Walk in the light! So shalt thou know
That fellowship of love
His spirit only can bestow
Who reigns in light above.
Walk in the light! And thou shalt find
Thy heart made truly his,
Who dwells in cloudless light enshrined
In whom no darkness is.

145

Walk in the light! And thou shalt own
Thy darkness passed away,
Because that light hath on thee shown
In which is perfect day.
Walk in the light! And thine shall be
A path, though thorny, bright:
For God, by grace, shall dwell in thee
And God himself is light.(27)

Liturgist: Make a joyful noise unto God, all ye lands.
Community: Let Psalms declare the glory of his name.

Community Right: God, give your own justice to the king,
your own righteousness to the royal son,
Community Left: so that he may rule your people rightly
and your poor with justice.
R: Let the mountains and hills
bring a message of peace for the people.
L: Uprightly he will defend the poorest,
he will save the children of those in need and crush their oppressors.
R: Like sun and moon he will endure,
age after age.
L: Welcome as rain that falls on the pasture,
and showers to thirsty soil.
R: In his days virtue will flourish,
a universal peace till the moon is no more;
L: his empire shall stretch from sea,
from the river to the ends of the earth.
R: The beast will cower before him
and his enemies will grovel in the dust;
L: the kings of Tarshish and of the islands
will pay him tribute.
R: The kings of Sheba and Seba
will offer gifts;
L: All kings will do him homage,
all nations become his servants.
R: He will free the poor man who calls to him,
and those who need help,
L: he will have pity on the poor and feeble,

and save the lives of those in need;
R: He will redeem their lives from exploitation
and outrage, their lives will be precious in his sight.
L: Long may he live, may gold from Sheba be given him!
Prayer will be offered for him constantly,
blessings invoked on him all day long.
R: Grain everywhere in the country,
even on the mountain tops,
L: abundant as Lebanon its harvest,
luxuriant as common grass!
R: Blessed be his name forever,
enduring as long as the sun!
L: May every race in the world be blessed in him,
and all the nations call him blessed!
R: Blessed be Yahweh, the God of Israel,
who alone performs these marvels!
L: Blessed for ever be his glorious name,
R: may the whole world be filled with his glory!
L: Amen.
R: Amen. (Psalm 72)

Liturgist: O Lord, I will meditate on your precepts.
Community: I will delight in your statutes; I will not forget your word.

OLD TESTAMENT LESSON: (Isaiah 60:1-6)

Liturgist: Incline your ear to me—
Community: And answer me when I call.

NEW TESTAMENT LESSON: (Matthew 2:1-12)
SILENCE
FREE PRAYER
APPOINTED PRAYER: (All)
     O God, by the leading of a star you manifested your only Son to
the peoples of the earth: Lead us, who know you now by faith, to your
presence, where we may see your glory face to face; through Jesus
Christ our Lord, who lives and reigns with you and the Holy Spirit,
one God, now and forever. Amen.(28)

Liturgist: May the God of patience and of consolation grant us to live together after the pattern of our Lord Jesus Christ, so that with one heart and one voice we may give glory to God, the Father of our Lord Jesus Christ.

Community: Amen.(29)

SEXT

Theme: The Baptism of our Lord — Time: 12 Noon-3:00 PM.
INVITATORY:

Liturgist: Come Holy Spirit,

Community: From heaven shine forth with your glorious light!

L: Come, Father of the poor; come generous spirit;

C: From heaven shine forth with your glorious light!

L: Most kindly, warming light! Enter the inmost depths of our hearts, for we are faithful to you.

C: Without your presence, we have nothing worthy, nothing pure.

L: Wash away our sin, send rain upon our dry ground, heal our wounded souls.

C: From heaven shine forth with your glorious light!

L: Let him who reigns from the throne, and to the Lamb,

C: Praise and honor, glory and power forever. Amen.(30)

HYMN:

Come Holy Spirit, heavenly Dove
With all thy quickening powers;
Kindle a flame of sacred love
In these cold hearts of ours.
Look how we grovel here below
Fond of these earthly toys;
Our souls, how heavily they go
To reach eternal joys.
And shall we then forever live
At this poor dying rate?
Our love so faint, so cold to thee
And thine to us so great!
Come Holy Spirit, heavenly Dove
With all thy quickening powers;
Come, shed abroad a Savior's love,

And that shall kindle ours.(31)

Liturgist: Make a joyful noise unto God, all ye lands.
Community: Let Psalms declare the glory of his name.

PSALM:
Community Right: Have mercy on me, O God, in your goodness,
in your great tenderness wipe away my faults;
Community Left: Wash me clean of my guilt,
purify me from my sin.
R: For I am aware of my faults,
I have my sin constantly in mind,
L: having sinned against none other than you,
having done what you regard as wrong.
R: You are just when you pass sentence on me,
blameless when you give judgment.
L: You know I was born guilty,
a sinner from the moment of conception.
R: Yet, since you love sincerity of heart,
teach me the secrets of wisdom.
L: purify me with hyssop until I am clean;
wash me until I am white as snow.
R: Instill some joy and gladness into me,
let the bones you have crushed rejoice again,
L: Hide your face from my sins,
wipe out all my guilt.
R: God, create a clean heart in me,
put into me a new and constant spirit,
L: Do not banish me from your presence,
do not deprive me of your holy spirit.
R: Be my savior again, renew my joy,
keep my spirit steady and willing;
L: and I shall teach transgressors the way to you,
and to you the sinners will return.
R: Save me from death, God my savior,
and my tongue will acclaim your righteousness.
L: Lord, open my lips,
and my mouth will speak out your praise.
R: Sacrifice gives you no pleasure,

were I to offer holocaust, you would not have it.
L: My sacrifice is this broken spirit,
you will not scorn this crushed and broken heart.
R: Show your favor graciously to Zion.
Rebuild the walls of Jerusalem.
L: Then there will be proper sacrifice to please you
R: —holocaust and whole oblation—and young
bulls to be offered on your altar. (Psalm 51)

Liturgist: O Lord, I will meditate on your precepts.
Community: I will delight in your statutes; I will not forget your word.

OLD TESTAMENT LESSON: (Isaiah 42:1-9)

Liturgist: From the depths I call to you, O Lord:
—hear my cry!
Community: Let your ear be attentive to the words of my prayer.

NEW TESTAMENT LESSON: (Mark 1:4-11)
SILENCE
FREE PRAYER
APPOINTED PRAYER
O God, you are the unsearchable abyss of peace, the ineffable sea of love, the fountain of blessings and the bestower of affection who sends peace to those that receive it. Open to us this day the sea of your love, and water us with the plenteous streams from the riches of your grace. Make us children of quietness and heirs of peace. Enkindle in us the fire of your love. Sow in us your fear. Strengthen our weakness by your power. Bind us closely to you and to one another in one firm bond of unity, for the sake of Jesus Christ. Amen.(32)

Liturgist: May the Lord bless us and keep us; may Christ smile upon us and give us his grace; may he unveil his face to us and bring us his peace.
Community: Amen.(33)

NONE
Theme: The Transfiguration — Time: 3:00 PM.-6:00 PM.
INVITATORY:

Liturgist: Lord, how great is your love!

Community: In you is the source of our life.

L: By your light we see light.

C: Our Savior Jesus Christ has appeared!

L: The Lord has destroyed death; life and immortality shine forth.

C: By your light we see light.

L: Glory to the Father, and the Son and the Holy Spirit.

C: Grace has now been revealed, our Savior Jesus Christ has appeared.(34)

HYMN:
Crown him with many crowns,
The Lamb upon his throne;
Hark! How the heavenly anthem drowns
All music but its own.
Awake my soul, and sing
Of him who died for thee
And hail him as thy matchless King
Through all eternity.
Crown him the Lord of life,
Who triumphed o'er the grave
And rose victorious in the strife
For those he came to save;
His glories now we sing
Who died and rose on high,
Who died, eternal life to bring,
And lives, that death may die.
Crown him the Lord of peace
Whose power a scepter sways
From pole to pole that wars may cease
And all be prayer and praise;
His reign shall know no end,
And round his pierced feet
Fair flowers of paradise extend
Their fragrance ever sweet.
Crown him the Lord of love;
Behold his hands and side,
Those wounds, yet visible above
In beauty glorified.

151

All hail, Redeemer, hail!
For thou has died for me;
Thy praise and glory shall not fail
Throughout eternity.(35)

Liturgist: Make a joyful noise unto God, all ye lands.
Community: Let Psalms declare the glory of his name.

PSALM:
Community Right: Why this uproar among the nations?
Why this impotent muttering of pagans—
Community Left: Kings on earth rising in revolt,
princes plotting against Yahweh and his Anointed,
R: "Now let us break their fetters!
Now let us throw off their yoke!"
L: The One whose throne is in heaven sits laughing,
Yahweh derides them.
R: Then angrily he addresses them,
in a rage he strikes them with panic,
L: "This is my king, installed by me on
Zion, my holy mountain."
R: Let me proclaim Yahweh's decree;
he has told me, "You are my son,
today I have become your father.
L: —ask and I will give you the nations for your heritage,
the ends of the earth for your heritage,
the ends of the earth for your domain.
R: —with iron scepter you will break them,
shatter them like potter's ware."
L: So now, you kings, learn wisdom,
earthly rulers, be warned:
R: serve Yahweh, fear him,
tremble and kiss his feet,
L: or he will be angry and you will perish,
for his anger is very quick to blaze.
R: Happy all who take shelter in him. (Psalm 2)

Liturgist: O Lord, I will meditate on your precepts.

Community: I will delight in your statutes; I will not forget your word.

OLD TESTAMENT LESSON: (Exodus 34:29-35)

Liturgist: Loving Father, you transfigured your beloved Son and revealed the Holy Spirit in the bright cloud:
Community: Enable us to hear the word of Christ with faithful hearts.

NEW TESTAMENT LESSON: (Matthew 17:1-13)

SILENCE
FREE PRAYER
APPOINTED PRAYER: (All)
   O God, who on the holy mount revealed to chosen witnesses your well-beloved Son, wonderfully transfigured, in raiment white and glistening: mercifully grant that we, being delivered from the disquietude of this world, may in faith behold the King in his beauty; who with you, O Father, and you, O Holy Spirit, lives and reigns, one God, forever and ever. Amen.(37)
Liturgist: May the God of hope fill us with all joy and peace in believing through the power of the Holy Spirit!
Community: Amen.

(1) Mendelson, Edward, W.H. Auden: *Collected Poems,* Vintage International, Vintage Books, a division of Random House Inc., New York, 1991, p. 351.

(2) Brico, Rex, Taize: *Brother Roger And His Community,* Collins, London, 1978, p. 95.

(3) *Praise God: Common Prayer at Taize,* Oxford University Press, New York, 1977, p. 7.

(4) Underhill, Evelyn, *Worship,* Crossroad Publishing Company, 370 Lexington Ave., New York, NY 10017, 1989, p. 114.

(5) *Op. Cit.,* Brico, p. 171.

(6) *Ibid.,* p. 182.

(7) *Op. Cit., Praise God,* pps. 145-146.

(8) *The Book of Hymns,* The United Methodist Publishing House, Nashville, TN, 1964, #324.

(9) *Book of Common Prayer* (The Draft Proposed) of the Protestant Episcopal Church, the Church Hymnal Corporation, New York, 1976, p. 221.

(10) *Op. Cit., Praise God,* pps. 151-152.

(11) *Op. Cit., The Book of Hymns,* #431.

(12) *Op. Cit., BCP,* p. 221.

(13) *Op. Cit., Praise God,* pps. 161-162.

(14) *Op. Cit., The Book of Hymns,* #443.

(15) *Op. Cit., BCP,* p. 285.

(16) *Op. Cit., Praise God,* p. 165.

(17) *Op. Cit., BCP,* p. 289.

(18) Op.Cit., *Praise God,* p. 168.

(19) Op Cit., *The Book of Hymns,* #89.

(20) *Op. Cit., Praise God,* p. 178.

(21) *Op. Cit., BCP, Te Deum Ladamus,* pps. 95-96, and *Suffrage B,* p. 98.

(22) *Op. Cit., Praise God,* p. 214.

(23) *Op. Cit., The Book of Hymns,* #464.

(24) *Op. Cit., Praise God,* pps. 124-215.

(25) *Op. Cit., BCP,* p. 217.

(26) *Op. Cit., Praise God,* p. 105.

(27) *Op. Cit., The Book of Hymns,* #403.

(28) *Op. Cit., BCP,* p. 214.

(29) *Op. Cit., Praise God,* p. 107.

(30) *Ibid.,* p. 316.

(31) *Op. Cit., The Book of Hymns,* #134.

(32) Lindemann, Herbert (Ed.), *The Daily Office,* Concordia Publishing House, St. Louis, 1965, pps. 96-97.

(33) *Op. Cit., Praise God,* p. 83.

(34) Adapted from *Praise God,* pps. 300-301.

(35) *Op. Cit., The Book of Hymns,* #455.

(36) *Op. Cit., Praise God,* p. 301.

(37) *Op. Cit., BCP,* p. 243.

BEYOND THE MYSTIC MOMENT

For one who has embarked upon the way of Christian perfection, God and Christ are no longer mere objects of belief, but personal realities apprehended within the deepest self. This apprehension calls the spiritual traveler toward a life so lived in response to the demands of constant communion with God, that he or she may say with Paul, "The life I now live is not my own life, but the life which Christ lives in me." (Gal. 2:20) While this state may be called one of self-awareness, or self-knowledge, it is far removed from the "self-esteem" advocated and promoted by the various human potential movements. This self-awareness or self-knowledge is a communion with the Living God within, whereas "self-esteem" is little more than blindness. The only "self" that concerns the spiritual traveler is the deepest self. Our other selves which are more or less wedded to the passions, are little more than testimonials to our as yet incompletely surrendered life.

The spiritual traveler must move toward the prize without knowledge of the roads, and must ask with Thomas, "How can we know the way?" (John 14:5) The way becomes clear only in those moments between communion with God and our response, when we experience on the one hand His intimate yet universal Presence, and on the other "the abject nothingness and self-abatement of the creature, thus brought face to face with the otherness and mystery of the Eternal."(1)

In Isaiah's encounter with the Presence he experiences both awestruck rapture and searing pain, and burning self-abasement as well as loving certitude. The narrative moves quickly to the response of faith which is submission, but this may not be so tidy a matter as the text would indicate. Instead of a symphony of movement from encounter to response, the mystic moment is more a sudden cacophony of messages from within: exaltation and alarm; bliss and self-loathing;

and soaring with the Psalmist on the wings of the morning even while sinking into the uttermost depths of the sea. This exalted self-abasement appears many times in the Psalms, perhaps nowhere more eloquently than here:

"I would not understand,
such a beast was I in your sight, O God.
Even so, I am always with you.
You hold my hand,
guide me with your counsel,
and in the end you will receive me with glory." (73:22-24)

In Paul's great mystic vision, (II Cor. 12:1-10) neither the glory nor the pain quickly subsided. He tells of being lifted up to the third heaven where he experienced things that he could neither understand nor tell, and, in the very next breath, speaks of something like a sharp physical pain—a thorn in the flesh—that would remain with him all his life, and would not be removed despite much prayer.

I had always taken the "vision" segment and the "thorn" segment as separate experiences. The question of what Paul's "thorn" may have been has always piqued my curiosity more than the reference to his mystic vision, and I suspect that I am not alone in this! I have come to believe, however, that they cannot be considered separately, but as part of the same encounter. This is holy compunction of the deepest sort, not unlike that compunction which Peter's preaching produced in Acts (2:37) where "they were cut to the heart." This compunction comes from the deepest self. The more intense the vision, the more violent the pain within.

When I was a student, I worked as a psychiatric aide in a large general hospital adjacent to a university. My role was a complex one: counselor and friend to the patients, keeper of the keys and the cigarette lighter, and a restraining influence upon the occasional patient who became unmanageable. There was an unlikely collection of individuals on my floor. Some were there for evaluation before being admitted to the state hospital. I suppose that I was there because of a secret pathology common to pre-ministerial students, which might be diagnosed as "needing to have all the answers."

One afternoon I took five of my charges on a field trip to the university library to view the Oriental Room which housed a valuable collection of teakwood furniture, jade and ivory carvings, brocades and rugs. I arranged the visit thinking that if these people were exposed to a little beauty—or a little culture—it might cheer them up. A fine idea that was! We were quite a collection ourselves: the arrogant pre-ministerial student, the Chippewa alcoholic prostitute, the failed farmer in for shock treatments, the politician's suicidal wife, the incorrigible teenage drug addict and the battered welfare mother.

The curator, in an expansive mood, took us up in the elevator and, opening the display cases, invited us to stroke a priceless Ming vase, manipulate a carved ivory sphere with smaller spheres on the inside, press a gold brocade against our cheeks and fondle a jade carving of a Samurai. It was quite a show, but it left the group more sullen than they had been before the excursion had begun. I myself was quite disappointed, because I had provided an encounter with more beauty than one might reasonably expect in the course of a single afternoon, or—I felt, self-justifiably—in an entire lifetime spent on the reservation!

Back at the hospital, the prostitute spoke first. "I didn't like it at all! I felt so dirty in that room! You know, just dirty!"

The farmer complained, "You could bust your butt all your life and never be able to afford anything in that room!"

The politician's wife agreed, "I know exactly what you mean! Another experience like that and I'll never be able to face my own house!"

Our encounter with the Presence of God may be like that field trip because it, too, overwhelms our restricted field of vision. It, too, is a judgment on our inability to do more than make a muddle of our life. It is a wound that comes from the deepest self, which punctures layer after layer of those false selves that we have permitted to control us. Our parents and grandparents may have called this "being slain in the Spirit." But whatever form it takes, we must cling to Christ, or the pain will be unbearable. If we are ever to move beyond the pain, and begin to travel the way of ascent, we must cry to Jesus with all our might, "Lord Jesus Christ, Son of God, have mercy on me a sinner." We must also accept His mercy when He gives it, or remain paralyzed in our sins.

The mystic moment reveals our painful servitude to the passions, or what the medieval church called "the capital sins." In an instant we see—perhaps for the first time—the festering thorn in our flesh, as clearly as if it had been illuminated by a surgeon's lamp. We see what it is that rankles us, tortures us, and undermines all our joy. We see

157

also that this thorn is so deeply embedded that it cannot be removed, at least in this life. We hear the voice of the Great Physician, speaking in compassionate tones, "No! My grace is all you need. My power is at its best in weakness."

Alexander Whyte, the gifted Scottish preacher of the last century, says this about Paul's servitude to this thorn:

"Greatest of all the apostles as he was; councillor almost of God Himself as he was; Paul's insight and faith and patience wholly failed him when his own thorn began its sanctifying work within him. You never made a greater mistake yourself than Paul made. With all his boasted knowledge of the mind of Christ, there was not a catechumen in Corinth...with more of a fretful child within him than the so-called great apostle was when this thorn came into his flesh."(2)

Why one is more susceptible to one of the passions than to another may be beyond our knowing. One is tortured by that spiritual pride which often comes as he or she makes progress in the way. Another may be tormented by envy toward those who seem more firmly advanced. Another, frustrated by the twists and turns of the journey, may be blinded by covetousness for those dubious blessings that seem more attainable than the seemingly illusory blessings of the Spirit. Another may fall into that paradoxical passion which is slothfulness, which persuades the traveler that the journey is not worth the effort. Then there are gluttony and lust. These, being the least spiritual of the passions, are also the most common, and hobble the spiritual traveler before he or she may even make a good beginning on the way. The many who assent to the rule of these passions do so because the Light does not blind and the pain is not so intensely felt in the self-gratifying dark. Their prayer is right out of W.H. Auden's *For the Time Being:*

Lead us into temptation
and evil,
for our sake!(3)

Evelyn Underhill says of Paul: "Grace is for him no theological abstraction, but an actual, inflowing energy, which makes possible a man's transition from the natural to the spiritual state."(4) The beasts have no need of grace because they fulfill the will of their Creator simply by being beasts. Men and women, on the other hand, having been endowed with an infinite capacity for Union with the Creator, cannot fail to notice this capacity unless they remain willfully blind. Even in the midst of this blindness, every person has, at one time or another, received an infusion of this Divine Light. There is grace in this light, and it gives us the capacity to approach our particular passion—our thorn—with utter clarity. It is this grace that causes us to see our thorn as a sanctifying work rather than an affliction that must be endured for its own sake. If we cannot yet name it as a sanctifying work, then we must wait in the faith that this grace—this divine energy—will come. It was about this energy and this pain that Charles Wesley composed the following lines:

"I want a principle within of watchful, godly fear,

A sensibility of sin, a pain to feel it near.

Help me the first approach to feel of pride or wrong desire,

To catch the wandering of my will, and quench the kindling fire.

If to the right or left I stray, That moment, Lord, reprove,

And let me weep my life away for having grieved thy love.

Give me to feel an idle thought as actual wickedness,

And mourn for the minutest fault in exquisite distress.

From thee that I no more may stray, No more thy goodness grieve,

Grant me the filial awe, I pray, the tender conscience give;

Quick as the apple of an eye, O God, my conscience make!

Awake my soul when sin is nigh, And keep it still awake.

Almighty God of truth and love, To me thy power impart;

The burden from my soul remove, The hardness of my heart.

O may the least omission pain My reawakened soul,

And drive me to that grace again, Which makes the wounded whole."

(1) Underhill, Evelyn, Mystics of the Church, Morehouse-Barlow Co., Inc., 78 Danbury Road, Wilton Connecticut 06897, Copyright, James Clarke and Co. Ltd., 1925, p. 33.

(2) Whyte, Alexander, D.D., Bible Characters In One Volume, Zondervan Publishing House, Grand Rapids, Michigan 49506, 1978, pps. 255-256.

(3) Mendelson, Edward, W.H. Auden: Collected Poems, Vintage International, Vintage Books, a division of Random House Inc., New York, 1991, p. 400.

(4) Op. Cit., Underhill, p. 48.